SAUCES

SALSAS, DRESSINGS AND DIPS

SAUCES

SALSAS, DRESSINGS AND DIPS

THE ART OF SAUCE MAKING: TRANSFORM YOUR COOKING WITH 150 DELICIOUS IDEAS FOR EVERY KIND OF DISH, SHOWN IN 300 STUNNING PHOTOGRAPHS

Contributing Editor Christine France

LORENZ BOOKS

This edition is published by Lorenz Books, an imprint of Anness Publishing Ltd, Blaby Road, Wigston, Leicestershire LE18 4SE; info@anness.com

www.lorenzbooks.com; www.annesspublishing.com

If you like the images in this book and would like to investigate using them for publishing, promotions or advertising, please visit www.practicalpictures.com for more information.

Publisher: Joanna Lorenz
Editor: Elizabeth Young
Designer: Ian Sandom
Production Controller: Christine Ni

A CIP catalogue record for this book is available from the British Library.

PUBLISHER'S NOTE
Although the advice and information in this book are believed to be accurate and true at the time of going to press, neither the authors nor the publisher can accept any legal responsibility or liability for any errors or omissions that may have been made nor for any inaccuracies nor for any loss, harm or injury that comes about from following instructions or advice in this book.

ETHICAL TRADING POLICY
At Anness Publishing we believe that business should be conducted in an ethical and ecologically sustainable way, with respect for the environment and a proper regard to the replacement of the natural resources we employ.

As a publisher, we use a lot of wood pulp in high-quality paper for printing, and that wood commonly comes from spruce trees. We are therefore currently growing more than 750,000 trees in three Scottish forest plantations: Berrymoss (130 hectares/320 acres), West Touxhill (125 hectares/305 acres) and Deveron Forest (75 hectares/185 acres). The forests we manage contain more than 3.5 times the number of trees employed each year in making paper for the books we manufacture.

Because of this ongoing ecological investment programme, you, as our customer, can have the pleasure and reassurance of knowing that a tree is being cultivated on your behalf to naturally replace the materials used to make the book you are holding.

Our forestry programme is run in accordance with the UK Woodland Assurance Scheme (UKWAS) and will be certified by the internationally recognized Forest Stewardship Council (FSC). The FSC is a non-government organization dedicated to promoting responsible management of the world's forests. Certification ensures forests are managed in an environmentally sustainable and socially responsible way.

For further information, go to www.annesspublishing.com/trees

Front cover shows sour cherry sauce for venison – for recipe, see page 157.

NOTES
For all recipes, quantities are given in both metric and imperial measures and, where appropriate, in standard cups and spoons. Follow one set of measures, but not a mixture, because they are not interchangeable.
Standard spoon and cup measures are level. 1 tsp = 5ml, 1 tbsp = 15ml, 1 cup = 250ml/8fl oz.
Australian standard tablespoons are 20ml. Australian readers should use 3 tsp in place of 1 tbsp for measuring small quantities.
American pints are 16fl oz/2 cups. American readers should use 20fl oz/2.5 cups in place of 1 pint when measuring liquids.
Electric oven temperatures in this book are for conventional ovens. When using a fan oven, the temperature will probably need to be reduced by about 10–20°C/20–40°F. Since ovens vary, you should check your manufacturer's instruction book for guidance.
The nutritional analysis given for each recipe is calculated per portion (i.e. serving or item), unless otherwise stated. If the recipe gives a range, such as Serves 4–6, then the nutritional analysis will be for the smaller portion size, i.e. 6 servings. The analysis does not include optional ingredients, such as salt added to taste.
Medium (US large) eggs are used unless otherwise stated.
The very young, pregnant women and those in ill-health or with a compromised immune system are advised against consuming raw eggs or dishes and drinks containing raw eggs.

Contents

Introduction

Light or creamy, rich or tangy, fiery or mild: a sauce, salsa, dip, dressing or marinade will transform any dish from the ordinary to the simply divine. Choosing the correct sauce is all-important; however, it should enhance the dish it is served with, not overpower it.

A sauce can be many things to many meals – from the simplest aside to accentuate the taste of plain cooking, to the integral part of a more complex dish. Savoury or sweet, fragile or full of punch, the one characteristic shared by all sauces is their liquid content. Unlike dry toppings, spice mixes or rubs, sauces include some form of liquid, even if this is a fat, such as butter, that becomes liquid on heating. There may be hundreds of brands and types to buy but nothing competes with home-made sauces.

BELOW: *Teriyaki is a sweet and syrupy Japanese sauce that can be used with a variety of fish and meat dishes.*

CLASSICAL STANDARDS

Old-school culinary experts still classify sauces by techniques such as thickening, reducing or colour. While classical methods are still the essence of many sauces, there is now a more relaxed approach. The basic laws may still apply, but they have given rise to new, exciting interpretations.

WORLD INFLUENCES

The international food scene has changed sauces and their use. Hot or cold, sweet-sour or savoury-sweet, we are all aware of brilliant sauces that transform everyday foods into exciting international meals. Whether based on stock, butter, flour, egg, fruit or vegetables, sauce-making methods are now fused with all kinds of cross-cultural influences.

Some dishes, such as casseroles and braised dishes, generate their own sauce during cooking; others involve adding food to a prepared sauce for cooking. While cooking in a sauce is a great way of making full-flavoured dishes, serve-on sauces can bring different culinary personality. Cooked in advance, sauce accompaniments can be prepared using the cooking residue from roasting, pan-frying or braising. They may be based on a marinade or basting mixture. The simplest flavoured butters or oils can be served as sauces or dressings.

ABOVE: *A basic tomato sauce can be tossed with pasta or used on a pizza base.*

ABOVE: *Add herbs such as thyme and bay leaves to sauces for maximum flavour.*

ABOVE: *Sauces made from tart fruit, such as cranberries, are good with poultry or meat.*

COOK-AHEAD SIMPLICITY

Making your own sauces does not have to be laborious. Instead of buying mixtures laden with hidden fats, sugars, seasoning and artificial flavourings, pick up a few favourite recipes and some sure-winner tips from the chapters that follow. Use them as your everyday, hassle-free flavour makers. Soon you will gain the confidence to experiment with a whole host of exciting new twists on your culinary repertoire.

The majority of sauces can be made in advance, cooled and chilled in a covered container. Some can be made one or two days in advance, while others can be prepared up to a week ahead. All sorts of sauces freeze well, ready for thawing at the last minute in the microwave. Making a big batch of a favourite simple sauce and freezing it in portions is an excellent way to save time.

Seasonal fruit and vegetables can be used for sauces when they are at their best and least expensive. 'Fresh' sauces can be frozen for year-round use. Don't limit yourself to savoury sauces. Fruit purées, chocolate sauces and syrups are all suitable for chilling or freezing.

There is just one simple rule when making sauces ahead, and that's labelling. Always label your pot of sauce with its name, quantity and date. It is also worth stocking up on cook-in bags or containers that can go from freezer to microwave, steamer, double boiler or oven.

USING THIS BOOK

The following pages feature a superb collection of 150 recipes to tantalize your taste buds. Included are a variety of sauces and accompanying dishes from all over the world, all of which have been tested to ensure perfect results, so you don't have to be experienced with cooking sauces to get the most out of this book. The recipes range from simple sauces such as mustard and dill to delectable sweet sauces such as butterscotch sauce. Most of the recipes are intended for four people, but the quantities can easily be halved to serve two, or doubled for eight. At the back of the book, there is a guide to the basic sauce-making techniques, as well as useful ideas for quick recipes.

Classic savoury sauces and dressings

This collection of sauces forms the basis of a repertoire essential to every professional cook. The sauces encompass all the key techniques, from lightly whisked white sauces, creams and gravy to juicy tomato, chilli, and vegetable concoctions. There are also speedy recipes for making satay sauce as well as a creamy garlic mayonnaise.

Beurre blanc

This light sauce goes perfectly with poached or grilled salmon or trout.

SERVES 4

3 shallots, very finely chopped
45ml/3 tbsp dry white wine or court-bouillon
45ml/3 tbsp white wine vinegar or tarragon vinegar
115g/4oz/1/2 cup chilled unsalted (sweet) butter, diced
lemon juice (optional)
salt and ground white pepper

1 Put the shallots in a small pan with the wine or court-bouillon and vinegar. Bring to the boil and cook over high heat until about 30ml/2 tbsp of liquid remains.

2 Remove the pan from the heat and leave to cool until the reduced liquid is just lukewarm.

3 Whisk in the chilled butter, one piece at a time, to make a pale, creamy sauce.

4 Taste the sauce, then season with salt and pepper and add a little lemon juice to taste.

5 If not serving the sauce immediately, keep it warm over a double boiler set over barely simmering water.

Nutritional information per portion: Energy 236kcal/966kJ; Protein 0.6g; Carbohydrate 3.2g, of which sugars 2.4g; Fat 23.7g, of which saturates 15g; Cholesterol 61mg; Calcium 16mg; Fibre 0.5g; Sodium 176mg.

Hollandaise sauce

This rich, warm sauce goes particularly well with a light supper of poached fish.

SERVES 4

115g/4oz/1/2 cup unsalted (sweet) butter
2 egg yolks
15–30ml/1–2 tbsp lemon juice,
white wine vinegar or tarragon vinegar
salt and ground white pepper

1 Melt the butter in a small pan. Meanwhile, put the two egg yolks and lemon juice or vinegar in a bowl.

2 Season with the salt and pepper and whisk until the mixture is smooth.

3 Pour the melted butter in a steady stream on to the egg yolk mixture, beating vigorously to make a smooth, creamy sauce. Taste the sauce and add more lemon juice or vinegar if necessary.

Nutritional information per portion: Energy 245kcal/1006kJ; Protein 1.6g; Carbohydrate 0.1g, of which sugars 0.1g; Fat 26.4g, of which saturates 15.8g; Cholesterol 162mg; Calcium 17mg; Fibre 0g; Sodium 179mg.

Aioli

This creamy garlic mayonnaise is simple to make and delicious. Serve it with salads or as a dip with crudités or as a quick sauce for pan-fried salmon. Try to use extra virgin olive oil for this mayonnaise if you can – it has a rich flavour that really makes this sauce special.

SERVES 4–6

4 large garlic cloves, peeled
2 egg yolks
250ml/8fl oz/1 cup extra virgin olive oil
15–30ml/1–2 tbsp lemon juice
salt

1 Put the garlic cloves in a mortar, add a pinch of salt and pound to a smooth paste with a pestle.

2 Transfer the garlic paste to a bowl. Add the egg yolks and whisk for 30 seconds, until creamy. Whisk in a little of the olive oil, drop by drop, until the mixture begins to thicken.

3 Add the remaining oil in a slow drizzle until the mixture is thick and creamy. Then beat in the lemon juice and salt to taste.

4 Serve the aioli immediately or cover with clear film (plastic wrap) and chill in the refrigerator until ready to use.

Nutritional information per portion: Energy 400kcal/1646kJ; Protein 1g; Carbohydrate 0g, of which sugars 0g; Fat 7g, of which saturates 75g; Cholesterol 10mg; Calcium 10mg; Fibre 0.1g; Sodium 100mg.

Roasted garlic sauce

A roasted garlic sauce has plenty of robust flavour without the harshness of some uncooked garlic sauces and dressings. This one keeps well in the refrigerator for several days. Serve it as an accompaniment to barbecued burgers or sausages, grilled steaks, lamb chops or pork steaks.

SERVES 6–8

6 large heads of garlic
120ml/4fl oz/½ cup extra virgin olive oil
2 thick slices white bread, about 90g/3½oz
30–45ml/2–3 tbsp lemon juice
salt and ground black pepper

1 Preheat the oven to 200°C/400°F/Gas 6. Slice the tops off the garlic and place the bulbs on a sheet of foil. Spoon over 30ml/2 tbsp of the oil and sprinkle with salt. Wrap the foil over the garlic and bake for 1 hour, until soft. Open out the foil and leave the garlic to cool.

2 Discard the crusts from the bread. Soak the bread in water for 1 minute, then squeeze dry.

3 Place the bread in a food processor with the garlic flesh, and process to a smooth paste. Add 30ml/2 tbsp lemon juice with a little salt and pepper.

4 With the machine running, gradually add the remaining oil in a thin stream to make a smooth paste. Check the seasoning, adding more lemon juice if needed. Turn into a bowl, cover and chill until required.

Nutritional information per portion: Energy 184kcal/761kJ; Protein 3g; Carbohydrate 9g, of which sugars 1g; Fat 15g, of which saturates 2g; Cholesterol 0mg; Calcium 17mg; Fibre 1.1g; Sodium 100mg.

Watercress cream

The delicate green colour of this cream sauce looks wonderful against pink-fleshed fish, such as salmon or sea trout. The flavour is complementary, too.

SERVES 4

2 bunches watercress or rocket (arugula), trimmed of bruised leaves and coarse stalks
25g/1oz/2 tbsp butter
2 shallots, chopped
25g/1oz/1/4 cup plain (all-purpose) flour
150ml/1/4 pint/2/3 cup hot fish stock
150ml/1/4 pint/2/3 cup dry white wine
5ml/1 tsp anchovy extract
150ml/1/4 pint/2/3 cup single (light) cream
lemon juice
salt and cayenne pepper

1 Blanch the watercress or rocket in boiling water for 5 minutes. Drain, refresh under cold running water, and drain again in a sieve (strainer).

2 Press the watercress or rocket against the sides of the sieve with a spoon to remove excess moisture. Chop finely and set aside.

3 Melt the butter in a pan and fry the shallots over medium heat for 3–4 minutes, until soft. Stir in the flour and cook for 1–2 minutes.

4 Remove from the heat and gradually stir in the fish stock and wine. Return the pan to the heat and bring the sauce to the boil, stirring constantly. Reduce the heat and simmer gently for 2–3 minutes, stirring occasionally.

5 Strain the sauce into a clean pan, then stir in the watercress or rocket, with the anchovy extract and cream. Season with salt and cayenne pepper and lemon juice to taste. Serve immediately.

Nutritional information per portion: Energy 113kcal/464kJ; Protein 0.2g; Carbohydrate 0.2g, of which sugars 0.2g; Fat 24.5g, of which saturates 4g; Cholesterol 25mg; Calcium 13mg; Fibre 0.1g; Sodium 75mg.

Mustard mayonnaise

Some people find classic mayonnaise difficult to make, but this version couldn't be easier. The essential thing is to have all the ingredients at room temperature.

SERVES 4

1 egg, plus 1 egg yolk
5ml/1 tsp Dijon mustard
juice of 1 large lemon
175ml/6fl oz/¾ cup olive oil
175ml/6fl oz/¾ cup grapeseed, sunflower or corn oil
salt and ground white pepper

1 Put the whole egg and yolk in a food processor and process for 20 seconds. Add the mustard, half the lemon juice and a generous pinch of salt and pepper. Put on the lid, then process the mixture for about 30 seconds, until well mixed.

2 With the motor running, pour in the oils through the feeder tube in a thin, steady stream. When the oils are taken up and the mayonnaise is pale and thick, taste and add more lemon juice and seasoning if you like. Scrape the mayonnaise into a bowl.

Nutritional information per portion: Energy 619kcal/2545kJ; Protein 2.3g; Carbohydrate 0g, of which sugars 0g; Fat 67.7g, of which saturates 9.3g; Cholesterol 98mg; Calcium 13.2mg; Fibre 0g; Sodium 35mg.

Mustard and **dill sauce**

This fresh-tasting sauce is not as sharp as other mustard sauces. It is delicious served with gravadlax, fresh smoked salmon, grilled fish or fish cakes. It also makes a tasty dressing for chicken salads. For extra bite and interest replace the French mustard with wholegrain mustard.

SERVES 2

1 egg yolk
30ml/2 tbsp brown French mustard
2.5–5ml/½–1 tsp soft dark brown sugar
15ml/1 tbsp white wine vinegar
90ml/6 tbsp sunflower or vegetable oil
30ml/2 tbsp finely chopped fresh dill
salt and ground black pepper

1 Put the egg yolk in a small bowl and add the mustard with a little soft brown sugar to taste. Beat with a wooden spoon until smooth.

2 Stir in the white wine vinegar, then gradually whisk in the sunflower or vegetable oil, drop by drop at first, then in a steady stream. As the oil is added, the dressing will start to thicken and emulsify.

3 When the oil has been completely amalgamated, season the sauce with salt and pepper, then stir in the finely chopped dill. Cover the sauce and chill for 1–2 hours before serving.

Nutritional information per portion: Energy 358kcal/1475kJ; Protein 3g; Carbohydrate 3.2g, of which sugars 2.8g; Fat 37g, of which saturates 4.8g; Cholesterol 101mg; Calcium 53mg; Fibre 0.7g; Sodium 452mg.

Olive oil, tomato and herb sauce

This aromatic sauce is served warm, rather than hot, and makes a good accompaniment to grilled or poached salmon or trout. It tastes so great you'll want to provide plenty of bread or boiled new potatoes to mop up any sauce remaining on the plate.

SERVES 4

225g/8oz tomatoes
15ml/1 tbsp finely chopped shallot
2 garlic cloves, finely sliced
120ml/4fl oz/½ cup extra virgin olive oil
30ml/2 tbsp cold water
15ml/1 tbsp lemon juice
caster (superfine) sugar
15ml/1 tbsp chopped fresh chervil
15ml/1 tbsp chopped fresh chives
30ml/2 tbsp torn fresh basil leaves
salt and ground black pepper

1 Peel and seed the tomatoes, and finely dice. Set aside.

2 Place the chopped shallot, garlic and olive oil in a small pan over a very gentle heat and infuse (steep) for a few minutes. The ingredients should warm through, but definitely not fry or cook.

3 Whisk in the cold water and lemon juice. Remove from the heat and stir in the tomatoes. Add a pinch of salt, pepper and caster sugar, then whisk in the chervil and chives. Leave to stand for 10–15 minutes.

4 To serve, gently reheat the sauce, then stir in the basil.

Nutritional information per portion: Energy 194kcal/800kJ; Protein 0.8g; Carbohydrate 2.3g, of which sugars 2.2g; Fat 20.3g, of which saturates 2.9g; Cholesterol 0mg; Calcium 25mg; Fibre 1.1g; Sodium 9mg.

Classic bread sauce

A traditional accompaniment for roast game, chicken or turkey, bread sauce is a very versatile white sauce, and is usually served with the Christmas turkey.

SERVES 6–8

475ml/16fl oz/2 cups milk
1 small onion, stuck with 4 cloves
1 celery stick, chopped
1 fresh bay leaf, torn in half
6 allspice berries
1 blade of mace
90g/3½oz/1¾ cups day-old breadcrumbs from a good-quality white loaf
freshly grated nutmeg
30ml/2 tbsp double (heavy) cream
15g/½oz/1 tbsp butter
salt and ground black pepper

1 Place the milk, onion, celery, bay leaf, allspice and mace in a pan and bring to the boil. Remove from the heat and half cover the pan. Then set the milk mixture aside to infuse (steep) for 30–60 minutes.

2 Strain the milk and place in a food processor. Remove and discard the cloves from the onion. Add the onion and celery to the milk and process until smooth.

3 Strain the milk back into the pan and bring to the boil, then stir in the breadcrumbs. Simmer gently, whisking with a small whisk, until the sauce thickens and becomes smooth. Add a little extra milk if the sauce is too thick.

4 Season to taste with salt, pepper and freshly grated nutmeg. Just before serving, whisk in the cream and butter. Serve warm.

Nutritional information per portion: Energy 100kcal/419kJ; Protein 3.4g; Carbohydrate 11.6g, of which sugars 3.2g; Fat 4.8g, of which saturates 2.9g; Cholesterol 13mg; Calcium 88mg; Fibre 0.3g; Sodium 123mg.

Onion gravy

This makes a delicious, dark onion sauce to go with sausages, liver, toad-in-the-hole or pork chops; a mound of creamy mashed potatoes is the essential accompaniment.

SERVES 4

40g/1½oz/3 tbsp butter or beef dripping
450g/1lb onions, halved and thinly sliced
2.5ml/½ tsp brown sugar
45ml/3 tbsp plain (all-purpose) flour
400–500ml/14–17fl oz/1⅔–2 cups hot beef or vegetable stock
1 fresh thyme sprig
10ml/2 tsp dark soy sauce
5ml/1 tsp Worcestershire sauce (optional)
salt and ground black pepper

1 Melt the butter or dripping over low heat. Add the sliced onions and fry, stirring occasionally, for 15–20 minutes, until softened.

2 Add the sugar, increase the heat a little and cook for 20–30 minutes, until the onions are dark brown.

3 Stir in the flour, cook for a few minutes, stirring, then gradually stir in 400ml/14fl oz/1⅔ cups of the hot stock.

4 Simmer, stirring, to make a thickened gravy, adding a little more stock if the gravy is too thick.

5 Add the thyme, season lightly, then cook gently, stirring frequently, for 10–15 minutes.

6 Stir in the soy sauce, and, if using, the Worcestershire sauce. Add more seasoning, if required, and a little more stock if the gravy is too thick. Remove the thyme, and serve.

Nutritional information per portion: Energy 636kcal/2648kJ; Protein 10.8g; Carbohydrate 75.8g, of which sugars 3.2g; Fat 34.4g, of which saturates 20.9g; Cholesterol 85mg; Calcium 189mg; Fibre 7.7g; Sodium 2393mg.

Apple sauce

This tart purée is usually served warm or cold, rather than hot. It is the classic accompaniment for roast pork, duck or goose, but is also good with grilled sausages, cold meats and savoury pies.

SERVES 6

225g/8oz tart cooking apples
30ml/2 tbsp water
thin strip of lemon rind
15ml/1 tbsp butter
15–30ml/1–2 tbsp caster (superfine) sugar

1 Peel the apples and remove the core. Cut into quarters then thinly slice.

2 Place the thin apple slices in a pan with the water and lemon rind. Cook over gentle heat, stirring frequently, until pulpy.

3 Remove and discard the lemon rind. Use a wooden spoon to beat the apple mixture until smooth or press it through a sieve (strainer).

4 Stir the butter into the apple sauce and then add sugar to taste.

Nutritional information per portion: Energy 42kcal/175kJ; Protein 0.1g; Carbohydrate 6g, of which sugars 6g; Fat 2.1g, of which saturates 1.3g; Cholesterol 5mg; Calcium 3mg; Fibre 0.6g; Sodium 16mg.

Cheese sauce

The mixture of flour and butter forms the basis of a white sauce. Adding cheese sauce to cauliflower in this way has become a staple of English cookery, and is a very popular dish.

SERVES 4

1 medium cauliflower, trimmed and cut into florets

FOR THE SAUCE

25g/1oz/2 tbsp butter
25g/1oz/1/4 cup plain (all-purpose) flour
300ml/1/2 pint/1 1/4 cups milk
115g/4oz mature (sharp) Cheddar or Cheshire cheese, grated
salt and ground black pepper

1 Bring a pan of lightly salted water to the boil, and cook the cauliflower for 5–8 minutes until tender. Drain and transfer the florets to an ovenproof dish.

2 To make the sauce, melt the butter in a pan, stir in the flour and cook gently, stirring constantly, for about 1 minute (do not allow it to brown).

3 Remove from the heat and gradually stir in the milk. Return the pan to the heat and cook, stirring, until the mixture thickens and comes to the boil. Then simmer gently for 1–2 minutes.

4 Stir in three-quarters of the cheese and season to taste. Spoon the sauce over the cauliflower and scatter the remaining cheese on top. Place under a hot grill (broiler) until golden brown.

Nutritional information per portion: Energy 318kcal/1318kJ; Protein 17.4g; Carbohydrate 4.4g, of which sugars 3.9g; Fat 25.8g, of which saturates 16.3g; Cholesterol 71mg; Calcium 371mg; Fibre 1.8g; Sodium 453mg.

Harissa

This simplified version of harissa – the classic spicy North African sauce – is extremely quick to make. It can be served as a dip with wedges of Middle Eastern flat bread, as a condiment with couscous and other North African dishes, or as a flavouring to spice up meat and vegetable stews.

SERVES 6–8

45ml/3 tbsp paprika
2.5–5ml/1/2–1 tsp cayenne pepper
1.5ml/1/4 tsp ground cumin
250ml/8fl oz/1 cup water
juice of 1/4–1/2 lemon
salt

1 Put the paprika, cayenne pepper, ground cumin and the water in a large, heavy pan, season with salt to taste, and bring to the boil.

2 Once boiling, remove immediately from the heat. Stir in the lemon juice to taste and allow to cool completely before serving or using.

Nutritional information per portion: Energy 35kcal/148kJ; Protein 2g; Carbohydrate 4g, of which sugars 0g; Fat 2g, of which saturates 0g; Cholesterol 0mg; Calcium 23mg; Fibre 0g; Sodium 100mg.

Chilli sauce

This version of chilli sauce gets its fiery flavour from the red-hot chillies and pungent garlic, and is fragranced with lots of exotic cardamom. This makes a delicious accompaniment to rice, couscous, soup, chicken or other meats. It can be stored in the refrigerator for up to 2 weeks.

MAKES ABOUT 475ML/16FL OZ/2 CUPS

5–8 garlic cloves, chopped
2–3 medium-hot chillies, such as jalapeño
5 fresh or canned tomatoes, diced
1 small bunch coriander (cilantro), roughly chopped
1 small bunch parsley, chopped
30ml/2 tbsp extra virgin olive oil
10ml/2 tsp ground cumin
2.5ml/½ tsp turmeric
2.5ml/½ tsp curry powder
seeds from 3–5 cardamom pods
juice of ½ lemon
pinch of sugar, if necessary
salt

1 Put all the ingredients except the sugar and salt in a food processor or blender. Process until combined, then season with sugar and salt.

2 Pour the sauce into a small serving bowl, cover with clear film (plastic wrap) and chill in the refrigerator until ready to serve.

Nutritional information per portion: Energy 326kcal/1361kJ; Protein 7.1g; Carbohydrate 21.4g, of which sugars 17.5g; Fat 24.3g, of which saturates 3.7g; Cholesterol 0mg; Calcium 142mg; Fibre 8.6g; Sodium 63mg.

Sweet and **sour sauce**

Serve this sauce poured over fried poultry, or use it as a base for any sweet and sour recipe. It is a very familiar flavour for lovers of Chinese food, and really enlivens savoury rice-based meals.

SERVES 6–8

300ml/½ pint/1¼ cups water
30ml/2 tbsp sugar
45ml/3 tbsp tomato ketchup
15ml/1 tbsp lime juice
30ml/2 tbsp plum sauce
10ml/2 tsp cornflour (cornstarch)

1 Combine all the ingredients except the cornflour in a small pan and bring the mixture to a slow boil.

2 In a bowl or jug (pitcher), blend the cornflour to a paste with a little water, then add to the simmering mixture and cook, stirring well, until it is the consistency of pouring cream. Add more water if the mixture gets too thick.

3 Use as required, or store in the refrigerator until needed.

Nutritional information per portion: Energy 284kcal/1209kJ; Protein 1.1g; Carbohydrate 74.1g, of which sugars 64.4g; Fat 0.1g, of which saturates 0g; Cholesterol 0mg; Calcium 27mg; Fibre 0.4g; Sodium 749mg.

Tamarind and **lime sauce**

This popular hot and sour dipping sauce is usually prepared for eating with freshly steamed shellfish or grilled fish. If you cannot find kalamansi limes, simply use the best limes you can buy.

SERVES 4–6

2 spring onions (scallions), white parts only
2 fresh red chillies
juice of 2 kalamansi limes
30ml/2 tbsp tamarind paste

1 Finely chop the spring onions. Carefully slice the chillies in half and remove and discard the seeds, then finely chop. Set aside.

2 Put the lime juice in a small bowl. Add the tamarind paste and mix together. Gradually add a little water to thin the mixture until it is of dipping consistency. Add the chopped spring onions and chillies and mix well.

3 Spoon the sauce into a jar or other suitable container with a lid, cover and store in the refrigerator for up to 1 week.

Nutritional information per portion: Energy 6kcal/23kJ; Protein 0.6g; Carbohydrate 0.6g, of which sugars 0.6g; Fat 0.1g, of which saturates 0g; Cholesterol 0mg; Calcium 10mg; Fibre 0.2g; Sodium 6mg.

Quick satay sauce

This version of the classic sauce is very easy to make and it tastes delicious. For parties, spear chunks of chicken with cocktail sticks and arrange around a bowl of warm sauce.

SERVES 4

200ml/7fl oz/scant 1 cup creamed coconut
60ml/4 tbsp crunchy peanut butter
5ml/1 tsp Worcestershire sauce
Tabasco sauce, to taste
fresh coconut, to garnish (optional)

1 Pour the coconut cream into a small pan and heat it gently over low heat, stirring occasionally, for about 2 minutes.

2 Add the crunchy peanut butter and stir vigorously until it is blended into the creamed coconut. Then add the Worcestershire sauce and a dash of Tabasco, to taste. Pour into a serving bowl.

3 Use a potato peeler to shave thin curls from a piece of fresh coconut, if using. Sprinkle the coconut over the dish of your choice and serve immediately with the sauce.

Nutritional information per portion: Energy 108kcal/451kJ; Protein 3.6g; Carbohydrate 5.8g, of which sugars 4.9g; Fat 8g, of which saturates 2.1g; Cholesterol 0mg; Calcium 30mg; Fibre 0.8g; Sodium 150mg.

Spicy peanut sauce

This is based on the famous Indonesian sauce that accompanies grilled pork, chicken or seafood. It can also be used to dress salads, and raw or cooked vegetables and fruit.

SERVES 4–6

30ml/2 tbsp groundnut (peanut) oil
75g/3oz/3/4 cup unsalted peanuts, blanched
2 shallots, chopped
2 garlic cloves, chopped
15ml/1 tbsp chopped fresh root ginger
1–2 green chillies, seeded and sliced
5ml/1 tsp ground coriander
1 lemon grass stalk, chopped
5–10ml/1–2 tsp light muscovado (brown) sugar
15ml/1 tbsp dark soy sauce
15–30ml/1–2 tbsp Thai fish sauce
105/7 tbsp coconut milk, plus 15ml/1 tbsp
15–30ml/1–2 tbsp tamarind purée
lime juice, to taste
salt and ground black pepper

1 Heat the oil in a frying pan and gently fry the peanuts, until they are lightly browned. Use a draining spoon to remove the nuts from the pan and drain thoroughly on kitchen paper. Set aside to cool.

2 Add the shallots, garlic, ginger, most of the sliced chillies and the ground coriander to the oil remaining in the pan, and cook over low heat, stirring occasionally, for 4–5 minutes, until the shallots are softened.

3 Transfer the spice mixture to a food processor or blender and add the peanuts, lemon grass, 5ml/1 tsp of the sugar, the soy sauce, the fish sauce and 105ml/7 tbsp of coconut milk. Blend to form a fairly smooth sauce.

4 Stir in the tamarind purée, taste and add more fish sauce, seasoning, lime juice and/or more sugar to taste. Stir in the extra coconut milk and a little water if the sauce seems very thick, but do not let it become too runny. Garnish with the remaining sliced chilli before serving.

Nutritional information per portion: Energy 123kcal/513kJ; Protein 3.9g; Carbohydrate 5.8g, of which sugars 4.7g; Fat 9.6g, of which saturates 1.6g; Cholesterol 0mg; Calcium 34mg; Fibre 1.3g; Sodium 557mg.

French white onion sauce

This classic sauce is excellent with veal, chicken, pork or lamb. It is also good poured over sliced hard-boiled eggs or poached eggs and then browned under a hot grill.

SERVES 4

40g/1½oz/3 tbsp butter
350g/12oz onions, chopped
25g/1oz/¼ cup plain (all-purpose) flour
500ml/17fl oz/generous 2 cups hot milk or stock, or a mixture of both
1 fresh bay leaf
a few parsley stalks
120ml/4fl oz/½ cup double (heavy) cream
freshly grated nutmeg
salt and ground black pepper

1 Melt the butter in a pan. Add the onions and fry gently over low heat, stirring occasionally, for 10–12 minutes, until they are soft and golden. Stir in the flour and cook gently, stirring constantly, for 2–3 minutes.

2 Gradually stir in the hot milk or stock, and bring to the boil. Add the bay leaf and parsley. Part-cover the pan and cook very gently, stirring frequently, for 15–20 minutes. Remove and discard the bay leaf and parsley, then process the sauce in a blender or food processor if you want a smooth sauce.

3 Stir in the cream and reheat the sauce gently, then season to taste with salt and pepper. Add a little more milk or stock if the sauce is very thick. Season with grated nutmeg to taste just before serving.

Nutritional information per portion: Energy 334kcal/1384kJ; Protein 6.4g; Carbohydrate 18.2g, of which sugars 11.5g; Fat 26.7g, of which saturates 16.6g; Cholesterol 70mg; Calcium 16mg; Fibre 0.4g; Sodium 106mg.

Béarnaise sauce

For simple meat dishes, this herby butter sauce adds a note of sophistication without swamping grilled or pan-fried steak. It also enhances plain vegetables.

SERVES 2–3

45ml/3 tbsp white wine vinegar
30ml/2 tbsp water
1 small onion, finely chopped
a few fresh tarragon and chervil sprigs
1 bay leaf
6 crushed black peppercorns
115g/4oz/$^1/_2$ cup butter
2 egg yolks
15ml/1 tbsp chopped fresh herbs, such as tarragon, parsley, chervil
salt and ground black pepper

1 Place the vinegar, water, onion, herb sprigs, bay leaf and peppercorns in a pan. Simmer gently until the liquid is reduced by half. Strain and cool.

2 In a separate bowl, cream the butter until soft. Set aside.

3 In a bowl over a pan of gently simmering water, whisk the egg yolks and liquid until paler in colour and light and fluffy in texture. Do not allow the water to boil rapidly or overheat the egg mixture or it will cook and curdle.

4 Gradually add the creamed butter, half a teaspoonful at a time. Whisk until all the butter has been incorporated before adding any more. Add the chopped fresh herbs and stir in seasoning to taste. Serve warm.

Nutritional information per portion: Energy 335kcal/1378kJ; Protein 2.6g; Carbohydrate 1.9g, of which sugars 1.5g; Fat 35.3g, of which saturates 21g; Cholesterol 216mg; Calcium 38mg; Fibre 0.5g; Sodium 241mg.

Barbecue sauce

A wide selection of ready-made barbecue sauces are available in the supermarkets, but they really don't compare with the home-made variety. This quick and easy-to-make version can be used to transform baked ribs, grilled chicken, sausages or fish into an interesting meal.

SERVES 4–6

2 x 400g/14 oz cans chopped tomatoes with herbs or garlic
1 onion
15ml/1 tbsp black treacle (molasses)
45ml/3 tbsp Worcestershire sauce
salt and ground black pepper

1 Pour the cans of chopped tomatoes into a pan.

2 Finely chop the onion and add to the pan with the black treacle and Worcestershire sauce, then bring to the boil.

3 Continue to cook uncovered, until thick and pulpy, stirring frequently.

4 Season lightly with salt and plenty of pepper and transfer to serving dish, or use as a marinade. Serve the sauce warm or cold.

Nutritional information per portion: Energy 31kcal/132kJ; Protein 1g; Carbohydrate 7g, of which sugars 6g; Fat 0g, of which saturates 0g; Cholesterol 0mg; Calcium 42mg; Fibre 0.8g; Sodium 100mg.

Mixed herb and peppercorn sauce

This lovely sauce relies on absolutely fresh herbs (any combination will do) and good-quality olive oil for its fabulous aroma. Make it a day in advance, to allow the flavours to mingle. Serve the sauce with simply cooked fish such as salmon or with grilled beef or lamb steaks.

SERVES 4–6

10ml/2 tsp cumin seeds
15ml/1 tbsp pink or green peppercorns in brine, drained and rinsed
25g/1oz/½ cup fresh mixed herbs, such as parsley, mint, chives and coriander (cilantro)
45ml/3 tbsp lemon-infused olive oil
salt

1 Crush the cumin seeds using a mortar and pestle. Alternatively, put the seeds in a small bowl and pound them with the end of a rolling pin.

2 Add the peppercorns and pound a little to break them up slightly.

3 Remove any tough stalks from the herbs and place in a food processor.

4 Add the cumin seeds, peppercorns, oil and salt to the food processor and process until the herbs are finely chopped, scraping the sauce down from the sides of the bowl if necessary.

5 Turn the sauce into a small serving dish, cover with clear film (plastic wrap) and chill until ready to serve.

Nutritional information per portion: Energy 50kcal/207kJ; Protein 0g; Carbohydrate 0g, of which sugars 0g; Fat 6g, of which saturates 1g; Cholesterol 0mg; Calcium 15mg; Fibre 0g; Sodium 100mg.

Mint sauce

The combination of vinegar, sugar and fresh mint leaves creates a delightfully sweet-sour tasting sauce, which has long been a customary accompaniment to roasted lamb.

SERVES 6–8

large handful of fresh mint leaves
15ml/1 tbsp caster (superfine) sugar
45–60ml/3–4 tbsp cider vinegar or wine vinegar

1 Place the mint leaves on a small chopping board and sprinkle the sugar over. Finely chop the mint leaves with the sugar (the sugar draws the juices from the mint) and put the mixture into a bowl.

2 Add 30ml/2 tbsp boiling water (from the kettle) to the mint and sugar, and stir well until the sugar has dissolved. Add the vinegar to taste and leave the sauce to stand for at least 1 hour for the flavours to blend.

Nutritional information per portion: Energy 351kcal/1468kJ; Protein 36.9g; Carbohydrate 2.5g, of which sugars 2.5g; Fat 21g, of which saturates 9.8g; Cholesterol 143mg; Calcium 23mg; Fibre 0g; Sodium 202mg.

Seafood dressing

This quick and simple sauce, also known as Thousand Island dressing, transforms fresh cooked prawns to make a well-loved and flavoursome dinner-party appetizer.

SERVES 6

60ml/4 tbsp double (heavy) cream, lightly whipped
60ml/4 tbsp mayonnaise
60ml/4 tbsp tomato ketchup
5–10ml/1–2 tsp Worcestershire sauce
juice of 1 lemon
salt, ground black pepper and paprika
fresh prawns (shrimp), chopped lettuce leaves and lemon wedges, to serve

1 Mix the double cream, mayonnaise, tomato ketchup, Worcestershire sauce and lemon juice together in a bowl.

2 Season with salt, ground black pepper and paprika to taste. To serve, spoon the sauce into individual serving bowls filled with lettuce leaves, fresh prawns, and garnish each bowl with a lemon wedge.

Nutritional information per portion: Energy 460kcal/1895kJ; Protein 9.6g; Carbohydrate 0.4g, of which sugars 0.4g; Fat 46.7g, of which saturates 29.4g; Cholesterol 193mg; Calcium 83mg; Fibre 0g; Sodium 555mg.

Parsley-balsamic dressing

This dressing marries a fine mix of flavours. On its own, this dressing goes perfectly with a vegetarian salad, and it is also delicious drizzled over grilled meat, such as lamb.

SERVES 4–6

45ml/3 tbsp olive oil
1 lemon
45ml/3 tbsp fresh flat leaf parsley
30ml/2 tbsp balsamic vinegar
salt and ground black pepper

1 Put the olive oil in a bowl. Cut the lemon in half and squeeze the juice into the bowl. Gently whisk the oil and lemon juice together well.

2 Roughly chop the fresh parsley and add this to the oil and lemon mixture. Lightly stir in the balsamic vinegar and serve.

Nutritional information per portion: Energy 117kcal/485kJ; Protein 2.7g; Carbohydrate 14g, of which sugars 10.1g; Fat 6g, of which saturates 0.8g; Cholesterol 0mg; Calcium 66mg; Fibre 3.1g; Sodium 9mg.

Caesar salad dressing

In 1924, Caesar Cardini invented the classic Caesar salad at his restaurant in Tijuana, just south of the US border, and this creamy dressing has since become a much-loved classic.

SERVES 4–6

1 large egg
1–2 garlic cloves
4 anchovy fillets in oil, drained
120ml/4fl oz/½ cup olive oil
10–15ml/2–3 tsp lemon juice or white wine vinegar
salt and ground black pepper

1 Bring a pan of water to the boil and add the egg, then boil it for 90 seconds. Plunge the egg into cold water, remove the shell and place the egg in a food processor.

2 Peel and chop the garlic and add to the processor with the anchovy fillets and process together.

3 With the motor still running, gradually add the olive oil in a thin stream until all the oil has been incorporated and the dressing is thick and creamy.

4 Add the lemon juice or wine vinegar and season to taste with salt and pepper.

Nutritional information per portion: Energy 198kcal/824kJ; Protein 5.6g; Carbohydrate 13.8g, of which sugars 1.7g; Fat 13.8g, of which saturates 2.1g; Cholesterol 50mg; Calcium 64mg; Fibre 0.9g; Sodium 400mg.

Chive flower dressing

There is something very enjoyable about using edible flowering plants and herbs from the garden. Grabbing a handful of this herb or that flower is all part of the creativity of cooking, and can produce exciting and unexpected results in the simplest dressings or marinades.

SERVES 4–6

15ml/1 tbsp champagne vinegar
75ml/5 tbsp olive oil
45ml/3 tbsp chives
about 10 chive flowers
salt and ground black pepper

1 Place the champagne vinegar in a large bowl with the olive oil and whisk together well with a whisk or wooden spoon.

2 Use a sharp knife to roughly chop the chives, then add them into the vinegar and oil mixture. Add the chive flowers and lightly mix together well. Season and serve over the dish of your choice such as boiled new potatoes.

Nutritional information per portion: Energy 232kcal/970kJ; Protein 3g; Carbohydrate 26.2g, of which sugars 4g; Fat 13.5g, of which saturates 2.1g; Cholesterol 0mg; Calcium 14mg; Fibre 2.2g; Sodium 23mg.

Blue cheese and **walnut dressing**

The combination of blue cheese and walnuts is lovely in this simple, yet deliciously fresh-tasting dressing that is the perfect accompaniment to crisp green salads. For extra flavour, try toasting the walnuts first.

SERVES 4

45ml/3 tbsp walnut oil
juice of 1 lemon
115g/4oz blue cheese, cut into small chunks
75g/3oz/$^3/_4$ cup walnut halves
salt and ground black pepper

1 Place the walnut oil and lemon juice into a large bowl and mix together well. Whisk briskly until thick and emulsified.

2 To serve, pour the dressing over the salad dish of your choice, and sprinkle the blue cheese over, crumbling it slightly. Then sprinkle over the walnuts, breaking them up roughly in your fingers as you go.

Nutritional information per portion: Energy 415kcal/1726kJ; Protein 10.6g; Carbohydrate 26.6g, of which sugars 26.4g; Fat 30.3g, of which saturates 7.3g; Cholesterol 22mg; Calcium 286mg; Fibre 4.5g; Sodium 383mg.

Salsas and dips

Versatile and eclectic, these brilliant recipes suit all sorts of occasions, and the preparation is often not much more than a whizz in a food processor. There are classic dips for appetizers or light meals, punchy mixtures to serve at dinner parties with delicious dunkers, and refreshing blends to transform plain cooked foods into a fusion of flavours.

Hot mango salsa

For sweet, tangy results, select a really juicy, ripe mango for this salsa – it is not worth making the salsa with a firm, unripe mango as it will not taste as good. (Keep an unripe mango in the fruit bowl for a few days until it has ripened.) This fruity salsa is a delicious accompaniment to chicken.

SERVES 6–8

1 medium ripe mango
1 lime
1 large mild fresh red chilli
½ small red onion
salt

1 Hold the mango upright on a chopping board. Use a knife to slice from top to bottom on either side of the stone (pit). Score the mango halves and carefully turn inside out. Slice off the flesh and finely dice.

2 Finely grate the lime rind and squeeze the juice.

3 Use a sharp knife to slice the chilli in half and remove and discard the seeds, then finely shred the chilli.

4 Finely chop the onion and mix it in a bowl with the mango, lime rind, 15ml/1 tbsp lime juice, the chilli and a little salt. Cover and chill until ready to serve.

Nutritional information per portion: Energy 18kcal/76kJ; Protein 0g; Carbohydrate 4g, of which sugars 4g; Fat 0g, of which saturates 0g; Cholesterol 0mg; Calcium 6mg; Fibre 0.7g; Sodium 100mg.

Yellow pepper and coriander relish

Relishes are quick and easy to make and they are delicious with cold meats and cheese or as a sandwich filler. Here the ingredients are lightly cooked, then processed to a chunky consistency. Red or orange peppers will work just as well as yellow as they all have a sweet flavour.

SERVES 4–6

3 large yellow (bell) peppers
45ml/3 tbsp sesame oil
1 large mild fresh red chilli
small handful of fresh coriander (cilantro)
salt

1 Seed and coarsely chop the yellow peppers. Heat the sesame oil in a frying pan and gently cook the peppers, stirring frequently, for 8–10 minutes, until lightly coloured.

2 Meanwhile, seed the chilli and slice it as thinly as possible. Transfer the peppers and cooking juices to a food processor and process lightly.

3 Transfer half the peppers to a bowl. Using a sharp knife, chop the fresh coriander, then add to the food processor and process briefly.

4 Transfer the contents of the food processor into the bowl with the rest of the peppers and add the chilli and a little salt. Mix well, cover and chill until ready to serve.

Nutritional information per portion: Energy 77kcal/324kJ; Protein 1g; Carbohydrate 6g, of which sugars 5g; Fat 6g, of which saturates 1g; Cholesterol 0mg; Calcium 12mg; Fibre 1.7g; Sodium 100mg.

Classic tomato salsa

This is the traditional tomato-based salsa that most people associate with Mexican food. There are innumerable recipes for it, but the basic ingredients of onion, tomato and chilli are common to all. Serve this salsa as a condiment. It goes well with a wide variety of dishes.

SERVES 6

3–6 fresh Serrano chillies
1 large white onion
grated rind and juice of 2 limes, plus strips of lime rind, to garnish
8 ripe, firm tomatoes
large bunch of fresh coriander (cilantro)
1.5ml/¼ tsp sugar
salt

1 Use three chillies for a salsa of medium heat; up to six if you like it very hot. To peel the chillies, spear them on a long-handled metal skewer and roast them over the flame of a gas burner until the skins blister and darken. Do not let the flesh burn. Alternatively, dry-fry them in a griddle pan until the skins are scorched and blackened.

2 Place the roasted chillies in a strong plastic bag and tie the top of the bag to keep the steam in. Set aside for about 20 minutes.

3 Meanwhile, chop the onion finely and put it in a bowl with the lime rind and juice. The lime juice will soften the onion considerably.

4 Remove the chillies from the bag and peel off the skins. Cut off the stalks, then slit the chillies and scrape out the seeds. Chop the flesh and set it aside in a small bowl.

5 Cut a small cross in the base of each tomato. Place them in a heatproof bowl and pour over enough boiling water to cover. Leave for 30 seconds. Then lift out the tomatoes and plunge them into a bowl of cold water. Drain well. Remove the skins.

6 Dice the peeled tomatoes and put them in a bowl. Add the chopped onion, which should by now have softened, together with any remaining lime juice and rind. Chop the coriander finely and add to the salsa, with the chillies and the sugar. Mix gently until the sugar has dissolved and all the ingredients are coated in lime juice. Cover and chill for 2–3 hours to allow the flavours to blend. Garnish with the extra strips of lime rind just before serving.

Nutritional information per portion: Energy 168Kcal/697kJ; Protein 3g; Carbohydrate 11.9g, of which sugars 9.2g; Fat 12.4g, of which saturates 6g; Cholesterol 24mg; Calcium 94mg; Fibre 3.1g; Sodium 758mg.

Creamy pineapple and passion fruit salsa

Pineapple and aromatic passion fruit create a salsa that's bursting with fresh fruit flavour – great with barbecued pork or baked smoked ham. It also makes a luxurious dessert!

SERVES 6

1 small pineapple
2 passion fruit
150ml/¼ pint/⅔ cup Greek (US strained plain) yogurt
30ml/2 tbsp light muscovado (brown) sugar

1 Cut off the top and bottom of the pineapple so that it will stand firmly on a chopping board. Using a large, sharp knife, slice off the peel. Then cut off the soft flesh, discarding the woody core. Finely chop the flesh.

2 Cut the passion fruit in half, and use a spoon to scoop out the seeds and pulp into a bowl. Stir in the chopped pineapple and the Greek yogurt. Cover and chill in the refrigerator until required.

3 Stir in the muscovado sugar just before serving the salsa – if you add the sugar too soon, the salsa will become too thin and juicy.

Nutritional information per portion: Energy 78kcal/328kJ; Protein 2g; Carbohydrate 12.8g, of which sugars 12.8g; Fat 2.7g, of which saturates 1.3g; Cholesterol 0mg; Calcium 53mg; Fibre 1g; Sodium 20mg.

Mixed melon salsa

A combination of two very different melons gives this salsa an exciting flavour and texture. Try serving it with thinly sliced Parma ham or smoked salmon for an impressive appetizer.

SERVES 10

1 small orange-fleshed melon, such as Charentais
1 large wedge of watermelon
2 oranges

1 Quarter the orange-fleshed melon and use a large spoon to scoop out the seeds, and discard them. Use a large, sharp knife to cut off the skin. Dice the melon flesh.

2 Pick out the seeds from the watermelon, and remove the skin. Dice the flesh into small chunks.

3 Use a zester to pare long fine strips of rind from both oranges. Halve the oranges and squeeze out all their juice into a large bowl.

4 Add the orange-fleshed melon and watermelon to the bowl with the orange rind and juice, and mix well. Chill for about 30 minutes and serve.

Nutritional information per portion: Energy 58kcal/250kJ; Protein 1.1g; Carbohydrate 13.5g, of which sugars 13.5g; Fat 0.4g, of which saturates 0.1g; Cholesterol 0mg; Calcium 30mg; Fibre 0.9g; Sodium 25mg.

Mango and **red onion salsa**

This tropical salsa is very simple and easy to make. It is livened up by the addition of passion fruit pulp and zingy lime juice. This salsa goes well with salmon and poultry.

SERVES 4

1 large ripe mango
1 red onion
2 passion fruit
6 large fresh basil leaves
juice of 1 lime, to taste
sea salt

1 Holding the mango upright on a chopping board, use a large knife to slice from top to bottom on either side of the large central stone (pit). Score the mango halves deeply in both directions and carefully turn the skin inside out so the flesh stands out and slice the dice off the skin. Place in the bowl.

2 Trim away any flesh still clinging to the top and bottom of the mango stone. Peel and dice these trimmings and place in the bowl.

3 Finely chop the red onion and place in the bowl with the mango. Halve the passion fruit, scoop out the pulp, and add to the mango mixture in the bowl.

4 Tear the basil leaves coarsely and stir them into the mixture with lime juice and a little sea salt to taste. Mix well and serve the salsa immediately.

Nutritional information per portion: Energy 42kcal/178kJ; Protein 1.1g; Carbohydrate 9.7g, of which sugars 8.4g; Fat 0.2g, of which saturates 0.1g; Cholesterol 0mg; Calcium 18mg; Fibre 1.9g; Sodium 4mg.

Peach and cucumber salsa

Angostura bitters add an unusual and very pleasing flavour to this salsa. The distinctive, sweet taste of the mint complements chicken and other meat dishes.

SERVES 4

2 peaches
1 mini cucumber
2.5ml/½ tsp Angostura bitters
15ml/1 tbsp olive oil
10ml/2 tsp fresh lemon juice
30ml/2 tbsp chopped fresh mint
salt and ground black pepper

1 Using a small, sharp knife, carefully score a line right around the centre of each peach, taking care to cut just through the skin. Bring a large pan of water to the boil. Add the peaches and blanch them for 1 minute.

2 Drain and refresh the peaches in cold water. Peel off and discard the skin. Halve them and remove the stones (pits). Dice the flesh and put in a bowl.

3 Trim the ends off the cucumber. Slice it lengthways into strips, then finely dice the flesh and stir it into the peaches. Stir the Angostura bitters, olive oil and lemon juice together and then stir this dressing into the peach mixture.

4 Stir in the mint with salt and pepper to taste. Chill and serve within 1 hour.

Nutritional information per portion: Energy 49kcal/203kJ; Protein 1.1g; Carbohydrate 4.8g, of which sugars 4.7g; Fat 3g, of which saturates 0.4g; Cholesterol 0mg; Calcium 28mg; Fibre 1.4g; Sodium 5mg.

Guacamole

One of the best-loved Mexican salsas, this blend of creamy avocado, tomatoes, chillies, coriander and lime now appears on tables the world over. Bought guacamole usually contains mayonnaise, but this is not an ingredient that you are likely to find in traditional recipes.

SERVES 6–8

4 tomatoes
4 ripe avocados, preferably Fuerte
juice of 1 lime
1/2 small onion
2 garlic cloves
small bunch of fresh coriander (cilantro)
3 fresh red Fresno chillies
salt
tortilla chips or breadsticks, to serve

1 Cut a cross in the base of each tomato. Place the tomatoes in a heatproof bowl and pour over boiling water to cover. (If you prefer, add the tomatoes to a pan of boiling water, taking the pan off the heat.)

2 Leave the tomatoes in the water for 30 seconds, then lift them out using a slotted spoon and plunge them into a bowl of cold water. Drain and peel. Cut them in half, remove the seeds, then chop the flesh and set it aside.

3 Cut the avocados in half, then remove the stones (pits). Scoop out the flesh and process it in a food processor or blender until almost smooth, then scrape into a bowl and stir in the lime juice.

4 Peel and finely chop the onion, then crush the garlic. Add both to the avocado and mix well. Roughly chop the coriander and stir into the avocado mixture.

5 Remove the stalks and seeds from the chillies, then finely chop them and mix them into the avocado mixture, with the tomatoes.

6 Taste the guacamole and add salt if needed. Cover closely with clear film (plastic wrap) and chill for at least 1 hour. Serve the salsa with tortilla chips or breadsticks to dip. If well covered, guacamole will keep in the refrigerator for 2–3 days.

Nutritional information per portion: Energy 156kcal/645kJ; Protein 2.1g; Carbohydrate 3.7g, of which sugars 2.5g; Fat 14.7g, of which saturates 3.1g; Cholesterol 0mg; Calcium 26mg; Fibre 3.5g; Sodium 11mg.

Blue cheese dip

This dip can be made in minutes and it is delicious with pears or vegetable crudités, but its uses don't stop there. In fact, it's thick enough for shaping into little patties to serve as a relish on freshly grilled steak. Add extra yogurt or milk for a thinner salad dressing.

SERVES 4

150g/5oz blue cheese, such as Stilton or Danish blue
150g/5oz/2/3 cup soft cheese
75ml/5 tbsp Greek (US strained plain) yogurt
salt and ground black pepper

1 Crumble the blue cheese into a large bowl. Using a wooden spoon, beat the blue cheese until it has softened. Add the soft cheese and beat well so the two cheeses are blended well together.

2 Gradually pour in the Greek yogurt beating it into the cheese mixture. Use enough yogurt to give the consistency you prefer.

3 Season with lots of black pepper and a little salt. Chill the dip in the refrigerator until you are ready to serve it.

Nutritional information per portion: Energy 267kcal/1106kJ; Protein 12.1g; Carbohydrate 0.4g, of which sugars 0.4g; Fat 24.4g, of which saturates 15.4g; Cholesterol 62mg; Calcium 253mg; Fibre 0g; Sodium 595mg.

Garlic dip

Two whole heads of garlic may seem like a lot, but roasting transforms the flesh to a tender, sweet and mellow pulp. Serve with crunchy breadsticks and crisps. For a creamier dip, substitute the mayonnaise with natural yogurt or soft cheese.

SERVES 4

2 whole garlic heads
15ml/1 tbsp olive oil
60ml/4 tbsp mayonnaise
75ml/5 tbsp Greek (US strained plain) yogurt
5ml/1 tsp wholegrain mustard
salt and ground black pepper

1 Preheat the oven to 200°C/400°F/Gas 6. Separate the garlic cloves and place them, unpeeled, in a small roasting pan. Pour the olive oil over the garlic cloves to coat them evenly. Roast them for 20–30 minutes, or until tender and softened. Then set them aside to cool for 5 minutes.

2 Trim off the root end of each roasted garlic clove. Peel the cloves and discard the skins. Place the roasted garlic on a chopping board and sprinkle with salt. Mash with a fork until puréed.

3 Place the garlic in a small bowl and stir in the mayonnaise, yogurt and wholegrain mustard. Check and adjust the seasoning, then spoon the dip into a bowl. Cover and chill until ready to serve.

Nutritional information per portion: Energy 179kcal/741kJ; Protein 3.6g; Carbohydrate 4.9g, of which sugars 1.1g; Fat 16.5g, of which saturates 3.1g; Cholesterol 11mg; Calcium 38mg; Fibre 1.2g; Sodium 139mg.

Sour cream cooler

This cooling dip makes the perfect accompaniment to hot and spicy dishes. Alternatively, serve it as a snack or appetizer with the fieriest tortilla chips you can find.

SERVES 2

1 small yellow (bell) pepper
2 small tomatoes
30ml/2 tbsp chopped fresh parsley, plus extra to garnish
150ml/¼ pint/⅔ cup sour cream
grated lemon rind, to garnish

1 Halve the pepper lengthways. With a sharp knife, remove the core and scoop out the seeds, then cut the flesh into tiny dice.

2 Cut the tomatoes in half, then use a teaspoon to scoop out and discard the seeds. Cut the tomato flesh into tiny dice.

3 Stir the pepper and tomato dice and the chopped parsley into the sour cream and mix well.

4 Spoon the dip into a small bowl and chill for at least 30 minutes. Garnish with grated lemon rind and parsley just before serving.

Nutritional information per portion: Energy 204kcal/845kJ; Protein 4.2g; Carbohydrate 12g, of which sugars 11.7g; Fat 15.8g, of which saturates 9.6g; Cholesterol 45mg; Calcium 114mg; Fibre 3.2g; Sodium 48mg.

Tzatziki

This classic Greek dip is a cooling mix of yogurt, cucumber and mint, and is perfect for a hot summer's day. Serve with strips of pitta bread and chunks of grilled lamb.

SERVES 4

1 mini cucumber
4 spring onions (scallions)
1 garlic clove
45ml/3 tbsp fresh mint
200ml/7fl oz/scant 1 cup Greek (US strained plain) yogurt
salt and ground black pepper
fresh mint sprig, to garnish (optional)

1 Trim the ends from the cucumber, then finely dice. Set aside.

2 Trim the roots off the spring onions and peel the garlic. Then chop both very finely and evenly. Chop the mint.

3 In a bowl, beat the Greek yogurt until smooth, then gently stir in the chopped cucumber, onions, garlic and mint.

4 Add salt and plenty of ground black pepper to taste, then transfer the mixture to a serving bowl. Chill until ready to serve and then garnish with a small mint sprig just before serving.

Nutritional information per portion: Energy 65kcal/269kJ; Protein 3.8g; Carbohydrate 1.9g, of which sugars 1.8g; Fat 5.3g, of which saturates 2.6g; Cholesterol 0mg; Calcium 99mg; Fibre 0.7g; Sodium 40mg.

Spicy cajun dip

This piquant dip is fabulous drizzled over crisp potato skins. It can be put to dozens of other uses – try it with burgers, grilled chicken and salad in wraps, or canned tuna tossed with pasta.

SERVES 4

4 large baking potatoes
vegetable oil, for deep-frying
salt and ground black pepper

FOR THE DIP
250ml/8fl oz/1 cup natural (plain) yogurt
2 garlic cloves, crushed
10ml/2 tsp tomato purée (paste)
5ml/1 tsp green chilli purée or 1 small green chilli, chopped
2.5ml/½ tsp celery salt

1 To make the dip, mix together all the ingredients and chill.

2 For the skins, preheat the oven to 180°C/350°F/Gas 4. Bake the potatoes for 45–50 minutes until tender. Halve and scoop them out, leaving a thin layer in the skins.

3 Heat a 1cm/½in layer of oil in a large pan or deep-fat fryer. Cut each potato half in half again, then fry them until golden on both sides.

4 Drain on kitchen paper, sprinkle with salt and pepper and serve with a dollop of dip in each skin.

Nutritional information per portion: Energy 265kcal/1095kJ; Protein 3.8g; Carbohydrate 12.2g, of which sugars 5g; Fat 22.8g, of which saturates 2.9g; Cholesterol 1mg; Calcium 121mg; Fibre 0.8g; Sodium 350mg.

Hummus

This classic Middle Eastern dish is made from cooked chickpeas, ground to a paste and flavoured with garlic, lemon juice, tahini, olive oil and cumin. It is delicious served with toasted pitta bread.

SERVES 4–6

400g/14oz can chickpeas, drained
60ml/4 tbsp tahini
2–3 garlic cloves, chopped
juice of 1/2–1 lemon
cayenne pepper
small pinch to 1.5ml/1/4 tsp ground cumin, or more to taste
salt and ground black pepper

1 Using a potato masher or food processor, coarsely mash the chickpeas. If you prefer a smoother purée, process them in a food processor until smooth and creamy.

2 Mix the tahini into the chickpeas, then stir in the garlic, lemon juice, cayenne, cumin, and salt and pepper to taste. If needed, add a little water. Serve at room temperature.

Nutritional information per portion: Energy 142kcal/596kJ; Protein 7.1g; Carbohydrate 11.6g, of which sugars 0.4g; Fat 7.9g, of which saturates 1.1g; Cholesterol 0mg; Calcium 98mg; Fibre 3.7g; Sodium 149mg.

Red onion raita

Raita is a traditional Indian side dish that is usually served as an accompaniment for hot and fiery curries. It is also delicious served with poppadums as a dip.

SERVES 4

5ml/1 tsp cumin seeds
1 small garlic clove
1 small green chilli
1 large red onion
150ml/1/4 pint/2/3 cup natural (plain) yogurt
30ml/2 tbsp chopped fresh coriander (cilantro), plus extra to garnish
2.5ml/1/2 tsp sugar
salt

1 Heat a small frying pan and dry-fry the cumin seeds for 1–2 minutes, until they release their aroma and begin to pop. Then lightly crush them in a mortar and pestle. Alternatively, try flattening them on a board by using the heel of a heavy-bladed knife, which will crush them slightly.

2 Finely chop the garlic. Slice the chilli in half and remove the fiery seeds then chop the flesh finely. Chop the red onion.

3 Place the yogurt in a bowl and add the garlic, chilli and red onion, along with the crushed cumin seeds and fresh coriander. Use a wooden spoon to stir the ingredients until they are thoroughly mixed.

4 Add sugar and salt to taste. Spoon the raita into a small bowl and chill until ready to serve. Garnish with extra coriander just before serving.

Nutritional information per portion: Energy 32kcal/134kJ; Protein 2.6g; Carbohydrate 4.6g, of which sugars 4g; Fat 0.6g, of which saturates 0.2g; Cholesterol 1mg; Calcium 100mg; Fibre 0.9g; Sodium 36mg.

Taramasalata

This smoked mullet roe speciality is one of the most famous Greek dips. It is ideal for a buffet or for handing round with drinks. Breadsticks or crackers make good dippers.

SERVES 4

115g/4oz smoked mullet or cod's roe
2 garlic cloves, crushed
30ml/2 tbsp grated onion
60ml/4 tbsp olive oil
4 slices white bread, crusts removed
juice of 2 lemons
30ml/2 tbsp milk or water
ground black pepper
warm pitta bread, breadsticks or crackers, to serve

1 Place the smoked roe, garlic, onion, oil, bread and lemon juice in a blender or food processor and process briefly until just smooth.

2 Add the milk or water and process again for a few seconds. (This will give the taramasalata a creamier texture.)

3 Pour the taramasalata into a serving bowl, cover with clear film (plastic wrap) and chill for 1–2 hours in the refrigerator before serving. Sprinkle the dip with freshly ground black pepper just before serving.

Nutritional information per portion: Energy 190kcal/795kJ; Protein 8.4g; Carbohydrate 12.9g, of which sugars 1g; Fat 12g, of which saturates 1.7g; Cholesterol 95mg; Calcium 32.5mg; Fibre 0.4g; Sodium 162mg.

Sauces for pasta

Simple, essential and practical, these meal makers provide variety for all kinds of occasion, from light midweek suppers to sumptuous dinners. Once you've sampled home-made pesto or an easy tomato or white creamy sauce, you will never look back. Many of these sauces can be frozen too, and they make great use of seasonal produce.

Butter and herb sauce

You can use just one favourite herb or several for this speedy recipe. This rich and buttery sauce is one of the simplest ways to dress up pasta, and is also one of the tastiest.

SERVES 4

400g/14oz fresh or dried spaghetti alla chitarra
freshly grated Parmesan cheese, to serve

FOR THE SAUCE

2 good handfuls mixed fresh herbs, plus extra herb leaves and flowers to garnish
115g/4oz/½ cup butter
salt and ground black pepper

1 Cook the pasta in boiling, lightly salted water according to the packet instructions.

2 To make the sauce, chop the herbs coarsely or finely, as you prefer.

3 When the pasta is almost *al dente*, melt the butter in a large frying pan or pan until it sizzles.

4 Drain the pasta and add it to the pan, then sprinkle in the herbs with salt and pepper to taste. Toss over medium heat until the pasta is coated in butter and herbs.

5 Serve immediately in warmed bowls, sprinkled with extra herb leaves and flowers. Pass round some extra grated Parmesan separately.

Nutritional information per portion: Energy 562kcal/2362kJ; Protein 12.7g; Carbohydrate 74.8g, of which sugars 3.9g; Fat 25.7g, of which saturates 15.2g; Cholesterol 61mg; Calcium 68mg; Fibre 3.9g; Sodium 184mg.

Cheesy breadcrumb sauce

In southern Italy, breadcrumbs are often used instead of grated cheese on pasta, which makes a good substitute if you've run out of cheese. You can also fry the breadcrumbs for extra texture.

SERVES 4

450g/1lb/4 cups anelli or other pasta shapes

FOR THE SAUCE

60ml/4 tbsp olive oil
3 garlic cloves, chopped
225g/8oz fresh, ripe tomatoes, quartered and seeded
10 fresh basil leaves, torn into shreds
115g/4oz/2 cups coarse dried breadcrumbs
30–45ml/2–3 tbsp grated Pecorino or Parmesan cheese
60ml/4 tbsp chopped flat leaf parsley
sea salt

1 Pour the oil into a large pan and add the garlic. Fry for 2–3 minutes, then add the tomatoes and basil. Stir in salt to taste, then cover and simmer the mixture for 20 minutes on medium heat. Add water if the sauce becomes too thick.

2 Bring a large pan of salted water to the boil. Meanwhile, put the breadcrumbs in a small bowl and add the cheese and parsley.

3 When the tomato sauce is almost ready, add the pasta to the boiling water. Bring it back to the boil, then cook the pasta according to the packet instructions, until just tender, then drain and return to the pan.

4 Pour over the tomato sauce and toss well. Divide the mixture among four bowls, sprinkle each portion generously with the breadcrumb mixture and serve immediately.

Nutritional information per portion: Energy 650kcal/2748kJ; Protein 22g; Carbohydrate 107.7g, of which sugars 6.5g; Fat 17.6g, of which saturates 4.1g; Cholesterol 11mg; Calcium 230mg; Fibre 5.1g; Sodium 354mg.

Italian plum tomato sauce

This tasty sauce uses store-cupboard ingredients, which is time-saving if you have an elaborate pasta to make. Here it is served with ravioli filled with prosciutto and cheese. It can also be served with plain pasta or with all sorts of simply cooked fish, poultry or meat.

SERVES 4–6

500g/1¼lb fresh pasta dough with eggs
60ml/4 tbsp grated fresh Pecorino cheese, plus extra to serve

FOR THE FILLING
175g/6oz ricotta cheese
30ml/2 tbsp grated fresh Parmesan cheese
115g/4oz prosciutto, finely chopped
150g/5oz fresh mozzarella cheese, drained and finely chopped
1 small egg
15ml/1 tbsp chopped fresh flat leaf parsley, plus extra to garnish

FOR THE SAUCE
30ml/2 tbsp olive oil
1 onion, finely chopped
400g/14oz can chopped plum tomatoes
15ml/1 tbsp sun-dried tomato paste
5–10ml/1–2 tsp dried oregano
salt and ground black pepper

1 To make the sauce, heat the oil in a large pan, add the chopped onion and cook over medium heat, stirring frequently, until softened.

2 Add the tomatoes. Fill the empty can with water, pour it into the pan, then stir in the tomato paste, oregano and seasoning to taste. Bring to the boil and stir well. Then cover the pan and simmer for 30 minutes, stirring occasionally and adding more water if the sauce becomes too thick.

3 Put the filling ingredients in a large bowl and season to taste. Mix them together with a fork, breaking up the ricotta.

4 Using a pasta machine, roll out a quarter of the pasta into a 90–100cm/36–40in strip. Cut the strip into two 45–50cm/18–20in lengths.

5 Using two teaspoons, put little mounds of the filling, 10–12 in total, along one side of one of the pasta strips, spacing them evenly. The filling will be quite moist. Brush a little water around each mound, then fold the plain side of the pasta strip over.

6 Starting from the folded edge, press gently around each mound with your fingertips, pushing the air out at the unfolded edge.

7 Sprinkle lightly with flour. With a fluted pasta wheel, cut first along each long side, then in between each mound, to make small square shapes with the filling sealed in.

8 Put the ravioli on floured dish towels and sprinkle lightly with flour. Allow to dry while filling the remaining pasta, to make 80–96 ravioli altogether.

9 Drop the ravioli into a large pan of boiling, lightly salted water, bring the water back to the boil and boil for 4–5 minutes. Drain well. Spoon a third of the ravioli into a warmed bowl. Sprinkle with 15ml/1 tbsp grated Pecorino and pour over a third of the sauce.

10 Repeat the layers twice, then top with the remaining grated Pecorino. Serve immediately, garnished with chopped parsley.

Nutritional information per portion: Energy 474kcal/1988kJ; Protein 26.4g; Carbohydrate 43.2g, of which sugars 4.8g; Fat 23.1g, of which saturates 11.1g; Cholesterol 180mg; Calcium 369mg; Fibre 2.4g; Sodium 880mg.

Alfredo sauce

This simple recipe was invented by a Roman restaurateur called Alfredo. Today's busy cooks will find cartons of long-life cream invaluable for this type of recipe.

SERVES 4

350g/12oz fresh fettuccine

FOR THE SAUCE

50g/2oz/1/4 cup butter
200ml/7fl oz/scant 1 cup double (heavy) cream
50g/2oz/2/3 cup freshly grated Parmesan cheese, plus extra to serve
salt and ground black pepper

1 To make the sauce, melt the butter in a pan. Add the cream and bring to the boil. Simmer for 5 minutes, stirring constantly, then add the Parmesan cheese, with salt and ground black pepper to taste, and turn off the heat.

2 Bring a large pan of salted water to the boil. Drop in the pasta all at once and quickly boil.

3 Cook the pasta for 2–3 minutes, or according to the instructions on the packet. Drain well.

4 Turn on the heat under the pan of cream to low, add the cooked pasta all at once and toss until it is well coated in the sauce. Taste the sauce for seasoning. Serve immediately, with extra grated Parmesan handed around separately.

Nutritional information per portion: Energy 697kcal/2917kJ; Protein 16g; Carbohydrate 67g, of which sugars 3g; Fat 42g, of which saturates 26g; Cholesterol 107mg; Calcium 172mg; Fibre 2.7g; Sodium 200mg.

Carbonara sauce

An all-time favourite sauce that is perfect for spaghetti or tagliatelle. This version has plenty of pancetta or bacon and is not too creamy, but you can vary the amounts.

SERVES 4

350g/12oz fresh or dried spaghetti

FOR THE SAUCE

30ml/2 tbsp olive oil
1 small onion, finely chopped
8 pancetta or lean bacon rashers (strips), cut into 1cm/½ in strips
4 eggs
60ml/4 tbsp crème fraîche
60ml/4 tbsp freshly grated Parmesan cheese, plus extra to serve
salt and ground black pepper

1 Heat the oil in a frying pan, add the onion and cook, stirring, over low heat, for about 5 minutes or until the onion has softened. Add the strips of pancetta or bacon to the onion in the pan and cook for about 10 minutes, stirring almost all the time.

2 Cook the pasta in salted boiling water according to the instructions on the packet, until *al dente*. Drain well and turn it into the pan with the bacon and onion. Toss to mix.

3 Put the eggs, crème fraîche and grated Parmesan in a bowl. Grind in plenty of pepper, then beat the mixture together well. Turn the heat off under the pan and immediately add the egg mixture.

4 Toss vigorously so that it cooks lightly and coats the pasta. Taste for seasoning, then divide among four warmed serving bowls and sprinkle with black pepper. Serve immediately, with extra grated Parmesan offered separately.

Nutritional information per portion: Energy 673kcal/2822kJ; Protein 32.5g; Carbohydrate 66.4g, of which sugars 4.1g; Fat 32.8g, of which saturates 13.2g; Cholesterol 252mg; Calcium 246mg; Fibre 2.8g; Sodium 1106mg.

Classic pesto sauce

Bottled pesto is a useful stand-by, but it bears no resemblance to the heady aroma and flavour of the fresh paste, which is quick and easy to make in a food processor.

SERVES 4

400g/14oz dried pasta

FOR THE SAUCE

50g/2oz/1 1/3 cups fresh basil leaves, plus fresh basil leaves, to garnish
2–4 garlic cloves
60ml/4 tbsp pine nuts
120ml/4fl oz/1/2 cup extra virgin olive oil
115g/4oz/1 1/4 cups freshly grated Parmesan cheese, plus extra to serve
25g/1oz/1/3 cup freshly grated Pecorino cheese
salt and ground black pepper

1 Put the basil leaves, garlic and pine nuts in a food processor. Add 60ml/4 tbsp of the olive oil. Process until the ingredients are finely chopped, then stop the machine, remove the lid and scrape down the mixture.

2 Turn the machine on again and slowly pour in the remaining oil in a thin, steady stream through the feeder tube.

3 Scrape the mixture into a large bowl and beat in the cheeses with a wooden spoon. Taste and add salt and pepper if necessary.

4 Cook the pasta according to the instructions on the packet. Drain it well, then add it to the bowl of pesto and toss well. Serve immediately, garnished with the basil leaves and hand-shaved Parmesan.

Nutritional information per portion: Energy 713kcal/269kJ; Protein 24.1g; Carbohydrate 43.2g, of which sugars 2.7g; Fat 50.5g, of which saturates 11.6g; Cholesterol 35mg; Calcium 468mg; Fibre 2.1g; Sodium 385mg.

Wild mushroom sauce

This rich mushroom and garlic sauce is delicious with pasta for a main course. Remember to pick wild mushrooms only with expert guidance or buy them from a reliable source.

SERVES 4

350g/12oz fresh or dried fusilli, cooked

FOR THE SAUCE

150g/5oz wild mushrooms preserved in olive oil
30ml/2 tbsp butter
150g/5oz fresh wild mushrooms, sliced if large
5ml/1 tsp finely chopped fresh thyme
5ml/1 tsp finely chopped fresh marjoram or oregano, plus extra herbs to garnish
4 garlic cloves, crushed
200ml/7fl oz/scant 1 cup double (heavy) cream
salt and ground black pepper

1 Drain about 15ml/1 tbsp of the oil from the mushrooms into a medium pan. Slice or chop the preserved mushrooms into bitesize pieces, if they are large. Add the butter to the oil in the pan and heat until sizzling.

2 Add the preserved and the fresh mushrooms, the chopped herbs and garlic. Season to taste. Simmer over medium heat, stirring frequently, for about 10 minutes or until the fresh mushrooms are soft and tender.

3 As soon as the mushrooms are cooked, increase the heat to high and toss the mixture with a wooden spoon to boil off any excess liquid. Pour in the cream and bring the mixture to the boil. Season if needed.

4 Drain the pasta and turn it into a warmed bowl. Pour the sauce over and toss well. Serve immediately, sprinkled with chopped fresh herbs.

Nutritional information per portion: Energy 662kcal/2769kJ; Protein 12.7g; Carbohydrate 66g, of which sugars 3.9g; Fat 40.5g, of which saturates 21.7g; Cholesterol 85mg; Calcium 52mg; Fibre 3.4g; Sodium 63mg.

Tomato and chilli sauce

This is much-loved Italian speciality – the name for the sauce, all' arrabbiata, means rabid or angry, and describes the heat and fire that comes from the chilli.

SERVES 4

300g/11oz dried penne or tortiglioni

FOR THE SAUCE
500g/1¼lb sugocasa
2 garlic cloves, crushed
150ml/¼ pint/⅔ cup dry white wine
15ml/1 tbsp sun-dried tomato paste
1 fresh red chilli
30ml/2 tbsp finely chopped fresh flat leaf parsley, plus extra to garnish
salt and ground black pepper
grated fresh Pecorino cheese, to serve

1 Put the sugocasa, garlic, wine, tomato paste and whole chilli in a pan and bring to the boil. Cover and simmer gently.

2 Drop the pasta into a large pan of rapidly boiling salted water and cook according to the packet instructions, or until *al dente*.

3 Remove the chilli from the sauce and add the parsley. Taste and season. For a hotter sauce, chop some or all of the chilli and return it to the sauce.

4 Drain the pasta and transfer into a bowl. Pour the sauce over the pasta and toss to mix. Serve immediately, sprinkled with parsley and grated Pecorino.

Nutritional information per portion: Energy 304kcal/1295kJ; Protein 10.5g; Carbohydrate 60.3g, of which sugars 7.2g; Fat 1.5g, of which saturates 0.2g; Cholesterol 0mg; Calcium 51mg; Fibre 3.4g; Sodium 303mg.

Tomato and aubergine sauce

Full of flavour, this sauce goes well with any short pasta shapes. It can also be layered between sheets of pasta and cheese sauce to make a delicious vegetarian lasagne.

SERVES 4–6

350g/12oz cooked pasta shapes

FOR THE SAUCE

30ml/2 tbsp olive oil
1 small fresh red chilli
2 garlic cloves
2 handfuls fresh flat leaf parsley, coarsely chopped
450g/1lb aubergine (eggplant), chopped
200ml/7fl oz/scant 1 cup water
1 vegetable stock (bouillon) cube
8 plum tomatoes, peeled and chopped
60ml/4 tbsp red wine
5ml/1 tsp sugar
1 sachet saffron powder
2.5ml/½ tsp ground paprika
1 handful fresh basil leaves
salt and ground black pepper

1 Heat the oil in a large frying pan and add the chilli, garlic and one handful of chopped parsley. Pound the garlic cloves with a wooden spoon, taking care not to splash hot oil, as this will release their juices. Cover and cook over low to medium heat for about 10 minutes, stirring occasionally.

2 Remove and discard the chilli. Add the aubergine to the pan. Pour in half the water. Crumble in the stock cube and stir until it is dissolved, then cover and cook, stirring frequently, for about 10 minutes.

3 Add the tomatoes, wine, sugar, saffron and paprika with another handful of parsley, the basil and seasoning. Pour in the remaining water. Stir well, replace the lid and cook for 30–40 minutes, stirring occasionally.

4 Check the sauce for seasoning, then toss with the cooked pasta in warmed bowls. Serve immediately.

Nutritional information per portion: Energy 277kcal/1174kJ; Protein 8.8g; Carbohydrate 49.7g, of which sugars 8.3g; Fat 5.5g, of which saturates 0.8g; Cholesterol 0mg; Calcium 45mg; Fibre 4.7g; Sodium 18mg.

Capers and yellow pepper sauce

This simple recipe makes for a delicious and very attractive pasta dish. Only the sweetest, juiciest yellow peppers should be used to achieve the right intensity of sweet, slightly peppery flavour.

SERVES 4

400g/14oz cooked spaghetti

FOR THE SAUCE

1 large yellow (bell) pepper
120ml/4fl oz/½ cup olive oil
2 garlic cloves, lightly crushed
3 large, salted anchovies, washed, dried and boned
1 large aubergine (eggplant), peeled and cubed
275g/10oz ripe tomatoes, peeled, seeded and cut in quarters
4 black olives, pitted and chopped
4 green olives, pitted and chopped
8 fresh basil leaves, torn into shreds
15–20ml/3–4 tsp salted capers, rinsed, dried and chopped
sea salt

1 Roast the yellow pepper over a naked flame, turning it frequently until the skin blisters and is blackened all over. Put it in a bowl, cover the bowl with clear film (plastic wrap) and set aside.

2 Heat the oil in a pan and add the garlic. As soon as the garlic turns brown, lift it out and discard.

3 Add the anchovies to the flavoured oil and cook for about 2–3 minutes, mashing them with a spoon to a smooth brown purée.

4 Pull off the skin from the roasted pepper. Cut the pepper in half, remove the seeds and membranes and chop the flesh into small squares. Add to the anchovy purée with the aubergine and tomatoes.

5 Stir in the olives, basil and capers, with a little salt, if needed, to taste. Cover the pan and simmer until the vegetables are soft.

6 Put the cooked pasta into a warmed bowl. Pour over the sauce, toss to mix, and serve.

Nutritional information per portion: Energy 569kcal/2394kJ; Protein 14.4g; Carbohydrate 80.1g, of which sugars 9.1g; Fat 23.5g, of which saturates 3.2g; Cholesterol 0mg; Calcium 56mg; Fibre 5.6g; Sodium 384mg.

Bolognese sauce

This recipe will bring back happy memories of flat-sharing and communal eating. While it goes so well with spaghetti or tagliatelle, it tastes good with all sorts of pasta shapes.

SERVES 4–6

400–450g/14oz–1lb dried spaghetti

FOR THE SAUCE

30ml/2 tbsp olive oil
1 onion, finely chopped
1 garlic clove, crushed
5ml/1 tsp dried mixed herbs
1.5ml/1/4 tsp cayenne pepper
350–450g/12oz–1lb minced (ground) beef
400g/14oz can chopped plum tomatoes
45ml/3 tbsp tomato ketchup
15ml/1 tbsp sun-dried tomato paste
5ml/1 tsp Worcestershire sauce
5ml/1 tsp dried oregano
450ml/3/4 pint/scant 2 cups beef or vegetable stock
45ml/3 tbsp red wine
salt and ground black pepper
freshly grated Parmesan cheese, to serve

1 Heat the oil in a medium pan, add the onion and garlic and cook over low heat, stirring frequently, for about 5 minutes until softened.

2 Stir in the mixed herbs and cayenne and cook for 2–3 minutes more. Add the minced beef and cook gently for about 5 minutes, stirring frequently.

3 Stir in the canned tomatoes, ketchup, sun-dried tomato paste, Worcestershire sauce, oregano and plenty of black pepper.

4 Pour in the stock and red wine and bring to the boil, stirring. Cover, lower the heat and leave the sauce to simmer for 30 minutes, stirring occasionally.

5 Cook the pasta according to the instructions on the packet. Drain and divide among warmed bowls.

6 Taste the sauce and add a little salt if necessary, then spoon it on the pasta and sprinkle with a little Parmesan. Serve immediately, with extra Parmesan.

Nutritional information per portion: Energy 639kcal/2692kJ; Protein 30.9g; Carbohydrate 83.5g, of which sugars 11.5g; Fat 21.7g, of which saturates 7.1g; Cholesterol 53mg; Calcium 59mg; Fibre 4.2g; Sodium 312mg.

Spicy sausage sauce

Serve this rich and fiery pasta dish with a robust Sicilian red wine and a crisp, leafy side salad to complement the rich, meaty sauce. This sauce goes equally well with short shapes such as penne.

SERVES 4

300g/11oz cooked tortiglioni

FOR THE SAUCE

30ml/2 tbsp olive oil
1 onion, finely chopped
1 celery stick, finely chopped
2 large garlic cloves, crushed
1 fresh red chilli, deseeded and chopped
450g/1lb ripe plum tomatoes, peeled and finely chopped
30ml/2 tbsp tomato purée (paste)
150ml/¼ pint/⅔ cup red wine
5ml/1 tsp sugar
175g/6oz spicy salami, rind removed
salt and ground black pepper
30ml/2 tbsp chopped parsley, to garnish
freshly grated Parmesan cheese, to serve

1 Heat the olive oil in a flameproof casserole or large pan, then add the chopped onion, celery, garlic and chilli. Cook gently, stirring frequently, for about 10 minutes, until softened and lightly browned.

2 Add the chopped tomatoes, tomato purée, wine, sugar and season with salt and pepper to taste. Bring to the boil, stirring frequently. Lower the heat, cover and simmer gently, stirring occasionally, for about 20 minutes. Add a little water if the sauce becomes too thick.

3 Chop the salami into small bitesize chunks and add to the sauce. Heat through, then taste for seasoning.

4 Put the cooked pasta into a large bowl, then pour the sauce over and toss to mix. Sprinkle over the parsley and serve with grated Parmesan.

Nutritional information per portion: Energy 561kcal/2357kJ; Protein 19.9g; Carbohydrate 63g, of which sugars 9.5g; Fat 24.5g, of which saturates 7.4g; Cholesterol 36mg; Calcium 64mg; Fibre 4.4g; Sodium 829mg.

Pansotti with **walnut sauce**

Walnuts and cream make a rich and luscious sauce for stuffed pasta, particularly the types filled with cheese and herbs. Serve this indulgent dish with warm bread and a light, fruity white wine.

SERVES 4

350g/12oz cheese and herb-filled pansotti or other stuffed pasta

FOR THE SAUCE

90g/3½ oz/scant 1 cup shelled walnuts
60ml/4 tbsp garlic-flavoured olive oil
120ml/4fl oz/½ cup double (heavy) cream
salt and ground black pepper

1 Put the walnuts and garlic oil in a food processor and process to a paste, adding up to 120ml/4fl oz/½ cup warm water through the feeder tube to slacken the consistency. Spoon the mixture into a large bowl and add the cream. Beat well to mix, then season to taste with salt and black pepper.

2 Cook the pansotti or stuffed pasta in a large pan of salted boiling water for 4–5 minutes, or according to the instructions on the packet. Meanwhile, put the walnut sauce in a large warmed bowl and add a ladleful of the pasta cooking water to thin it.

3 Drain the pasta and transfer it into the bowl of walnut sauce. Toss well until thoroughly mixed, then serve immediately while hot.

Nutritional information per portion: Energy 550kcal/2282kJ; Protein 11g; Carbohydrate 24g, of which sugars 2g; Fat 47g, of which saturates 13g; Cholesterol 41mg; Calcium 136mg; Fibre 1.9g; Sodium 200mg.

Two sauces for **cannelloni**

The combination of tomato sauce and the creamy white sauce makes this cannelloni delicious. For a special occasion, make it in advance; then add the white sauce and bake on the day.

SERVES 6

15ml/1 tbsp olive oil
1 small onion, finely chopped
450g/1lb minced (ground) beef
1 garlic clove, finely chopped
5ml/1 tsp dried mixed herbs
120ml/4fl oz/½ cup beef stock
1 egg
75g/3oz cooked ham or Mortadella sausage, finely chopped
45ml/3 tbsp fine fresh white breadcrumbs
115g/4oz/1¼ cups freshly grated Parmesan cheese
18 pre-cooked cannelloni tubes
salt and ground black pepper

FOR THE TOMATO SAUCE
30ml/2 tbsp olive oil
1 small onion, finely chopped
½ carrot, finely chopped
1 celery stick, finely chopped
1 garlic clove, crushed
400g/14oz can chopped plum tomatoes
a few sprigs of fresh basil
2.5ml/½ tsp dried oregano

FOR THE WHITE SAUCE
50g/2oz/¼ cup butter
50g/2oz/½ cup plain (all-purpose) flour
900ml/1½ pints/3¾ cups milk
freshly grated nutmeg

1 Heat the olive oil in a pan and cook the chopped onion over gentle heat, stirring occasionally, for about 5 minutes, until softened.

2 Add the minced beef and garlic and cook for 10 minutes, stirring and breaking up any lumps with a wooden spoon.

3 Add the herbs, and season to taste, then moisten with half the stock. Cover the pan and allow to simmer for 25 minutes, stirring occasionally and adding more stock as it reduces. Spoon into a bowl and allow to cool.

4 To make the tomato sauce, heat the olive oil in a pan, add the vegetables and garlic and cook over medium heat, stirring frequently, for 10 minutes. Add the tomatoes. Fill the empty can with water, pour it into the pan, then add the herbs, and season to taste. Bring to a boil, lower the heat, cover and simmer for 25–30 minutes, stirring occasionally. Purée the tomato sauce in a blender or food processor.

5 Stir the egg, ham or sausage, breadcrumbs, 90ml/6 tbsp Parmesan and seasoning into the meat. Spread a little tomato sauce in a baking dish.

6 Use a teaspoon to fill the cannelloni with the meat and place in a single layer on the sauce. Pour the remaining tomato sauce over.

7 Preheat the oven to 190°C/375°F/Gas 5. For the white sauce, melt the butter in a pan, add the flour and cook for 1–2 minutes. Stir in the milk, then bring to the boil, stirring. Add nutmeg and season. Pour over the cannelloni, then sprinkle with Parmesan. Bake for 40–45 minutes and stand for 10 minutes before serving.

Nutritional information per portion: Energy 680kcal/2847kJ; Protein 38.2g; Carbohydrate 54.5g, of which sugars 12.5g; Fat 35.9g, of which saturates 16.4g; Cholesterol 130mg; Calcium 469mg; Fibre 2.8g; Sodium 615mg.

Creamy smoked trout sauce

The fennel and dill really complement the flavour of the smoked trout in this tasty dish and the little pasta shells catch the trout, creating scrumptious mouthfuls.

SERVES 8

450g/1lb/4 cups pasta shapes, cooked

FOR THE SAUCE

15g/½oz/1 tbsp butter
175g/6oz/1 cup chopped fennel bulb
6 spring onions (scallions), 2 finely chopped and the rest thinly sliced
225g/8oz skinless smoked trout fillets
45ml/3 tbsp chopped fresh dill
120ml/4fl oz/½ cup mayonnaise
10ml/2 tsp fresh lemon juice
30ml/2 tbsp whipping cream
salt and ground black pepper
dill sprigs, to garnish

1 Melt the butter in a small pan. Cook the fennel and chopped spring onions for 3–5 minutes. Transfer to a large bowl and cool slightly.

2 Flake the trout fillets and add to the bowl with the sliced spring onions, dill, mayonnaise, lemon juice and cream. Season and mix.

3 Add the cooked pasta to the sauce and toss the ingredients together to evenly coat with the sauce all over. Check seasoning and add more salt and pepper if necessary.

4 Serve immediately garnished with sprigs of dill. Alternatively, serve lightly chilled if you prefer.

Nutritional information per portion: Energy 369kcal/1548kJ; Protein 14.5g; Carbohydrate 42.7g, of which sugars 2.8g; Fat 16.8g, of which saturates 4g; Cholesterol 29mg; Calcium 31mg; Fibre 2.3g; Sodium 613mg.

Smoked salmon and mushroom sauce

The button mushrooms and smoked salmon combine beautifully in this modern day classic from Italy. It is very easy to make and perfect for a quick supper when you're short of time.

SERVES 6

350g/12oz cooked linguine or spaghetti

FOR THE SAUCE

30ml/2 tbsp olive oil
115g/4oz/1 cup button mushrooms, finely sliced
250ml/8fl oz/1 cup dry white wine
7.5ml/1½ tsp fresh dill or 5ml/1 tsp dried dill weed
handful of fresh chives, chopped
300ml/½ pint/1¼ cups low-fat fromage frais or cream cheese
225g/8oz smoked salmon, cut into thin strips
lemon juice, to taste
ground black pepper
whole chives, to garnish

1 Heat the oil in a wide, shallow pan. Add the sliced mushrooms and fry them over gentle heat for 4–5 minutes until they are softened but not coloured.

2 Pour the white wine into the pan. Increase the heat and boil rapidly for about 5 minutes, until the wine has reduced considerably.

3 Stir in the herbs and the fromage frais or cream cheese. Fold in the salmon and reheat gently, but do not let the sauce boil or it will curdle. Stir in pepper and lemon juice to taste.

4 Put the cooked pasta into a warmed serving dish and toss gently with the salmon sauce before serving, garnished with chives.

Nutritional information per portion: Energy 208kcal/874kJ; Protein 16g; Carbohydrate 15g, of which sugars 4g; Fat 7g, of which saturates 1g; Cholesterol 14g; Calcium 63mg; Fibre 0.8g; Sodium 725mg.

Sauces for fish and shellfish

Fish and shellfish have a delicate and distinctive flavour. These recipes show how to combine herbs and spices with the right type of sauce to complement the different types of fish and shellfish. Spicy and creamy, piquant with horseradish, lively with chilli, or aromatic with Chinese seasoning, there are plenty of options for producing wonderful meals.

Tartare sauce for fried sprats

This is an authentic tartare sauce to serve with all kinds of fish, especially fried, but for a simpler and quick version you could always stir the flavourings into some ready-made mayonnaise.

SERVES 4

8 sprats, cleaned, and top and tailed
60ml/4 tbsp chopped fresh chives
1 egg
45ml/3 tbsp milk
50g/2oz/½ cup rye flour
200g/7oz/4 cups fine fresh breadcrumbs
vegetable oil, for shallow frying
salt and ground white pepper

FOR THE SAUCE

2 egg yolks
15ml/1 tbsp mustard
15ml/1 tbsp white wine vinegar
200ml/7fl oz/scant 1 cup vegetable oil
5ml/1 tsp anchovy essence (paste)
15ml/1 tbsp chopped gherkin
15ml/1 tbsp chopped capers
15ml/1 tbsp chopped fresh parsley
salt and ground black pepper

1 To make the sauce, whisk the egg yolks, mustard and vinegar in a bowl. Slowly add the oil at first, then in a slow, steady stream, whisking all the time until it begins to thicken like mayonnaise.

2 Stir in the anchovy essence, chopped gherkin, capers and parsley into the sauce and season to taste with salt and pepper. Transfer into a suitable container and store in the refrigerator until ready to use.

3 Season the insides of the fish with salt and pepper and sprinkle over the chopped chives. Break the egg on to a plate and beat together with the milk. Spread the flour and the breadcrumbs on separate plates. Dip the fish in the flour, to coat on both sides, then in the beaten egg and finally in the breadcrumbs.

4 Heat the oil in a large frying pan, add the coated fish and fry for 5 minutes on each side until crisp and tender. Serve with the sauce.

Nutritional information per portion: Energy 592kcal/2466kJ; Protein 18.8g; Carbohydrate 39.2g, of which sugars 1.7g; Fat 41g, of which saturates 5.7g; Cholesterol 156mg; Calcium 141mg; Fibre 1.3g; Sodium 601mg.

Caper butter sauce for baked herrings

This recipe is a modern take on a traditional Finnish recipe using herrings. The flavour of the dill adds a refreshing touch to this otherwise simple dish.

SERVES 4

a little butter, for greasing
50g/2oz/1 cup fine fresh breadcrumbs
600g/1lb 6oz herring fillets
salt

FOR THE SAUCE
100g/3¾oz/scant ½ cup butter, softened
15ml/1 tbsp vodka
30ml/2 tbsp chopped fresh dill
15ml/1 tbsp capers
1 large pinch cayenne pepper

1 Preheat the oven to 200°C/400°F/Gas 6. Grease a shallow, ovenproof dish with butter and sprinkle 15ml/1 tbsp of the breadcrumbs over the base.

2 To make the sauce, put the softened butter in a bowl and beat until it is light and fluffy, then whisk in the vodka, dill, capers and cayenne pepper.

3 Season the fish with salt then fold each fillet in half, so that the skin sides are on the outside. Lightly press the folded fish together with your fingers. Arrange the fillets in the prepared dish.

4 Spread the sauce over the fish, then sprinkle over the remaining breadcrumbs. Bake the fish in the oven for 25 minutes or until the top is crisp and golden brown. Serve immediately while hot.

Nutritional information per portion: Energy 545kcal/2261kJ; Protein 28.6g; Carbohydrate 10.1g, of which sugars 0.7g; Fat 42.8g, of which saturates 19.3g; Cholesterol 134mg; Calcium 126mg; Fibre 0.7g; Sodium 444mg.

White wine sauce for fish dumplings

Served with fresh summer vegetables, this rich and creamy white wine sauce can accompany any white fish such as pike or perch, but it is best served with home-made fish dumplings.

SERVES 4

500g/1¼lb white fish fillets, plus their bones
2 egg whites
5ml/1 tsp salt
2.5ml/½ tsp ground white pepper
a pinch of cayenne pepper
cooked early summer vegetables, such as young carrots, peas, asparagus and spinach, to serve

FOR THE SAUCE

25ml/1½ tbsp vegetable oil
1 onion, chopped
1 small celery stick, chopped
300ml/½ pint/1¼ cups white wine
50g/2oz/¼ cup unsalted (sweet) butter
30ml/2 tbsp plain (all-purpose) flour
200ml/7fl oz/scant 1 cup double (heavy) cream
2 egg yolks
15ml/1 tbsp chopped fresh dill
salt and ground black or white pepper

1 Cut the fish into small dice, put in the bowl of a food processor and blend until finely chopped, slowly adding the egg whites, salt, pepper and cayenne pepper while blending. Put the fish paste in a bowl and place in the freezer for 20 minutes, until very cold but not frozen. Beat in 100ml/3½fl oz/scant ½ cup of the cream, then set aside in the refrigerator.

2 Heat the oil in a pan, add the onion and celery and fry for about 5 minutes, until softened but not browned. Add the fish bones and continue to cook for 10 minutes, until they start to smell cooked.

3 Pour in half of the white wine and enough water to just cover the bones. Bring to the boil, then reduce the heat and simmer for 20 minutes. Strain the stock through a sieve (strainer) into a clean pan. You should have about 400ml/14fl oz/1⅔ cups fish stock.

4 Bring the stock to a gentle simmer. Use two tablespoons to shape the fish mixture into balls and drop these into the boiling stock in two or three batches. Cook for about 5 minutes, turning them over gently during cooking. Using a slotted spoon, transfer to an ovenproof dish and keep warm.

5 To finish the sauce, melt the butter in a pan, stir in the flour to make a roux that comes cleanly away from the pan base as it is stirred, then stir in a ladleful of the fish stock.

6 Slowly bring to the boil, stirring all the time, until the sauce boils and thickens. Repeat the process until the sauce has a smooth, velvet texture.

7 Stir the remaining white wine and the remaining cream into the sauce, and bring to the boil then quickly remove from the heat. Whisk in the egg yolks and the chopped dill, then taste and season with salt and pepper according to taste. Pour the sauce over the dumplings and serve hot, on a bed of cooked early summer vegetables, if you like.

Nutritional information per portion: Energy 600kcal/2484kJ; Protein 27.7g; Carbohydrate 6.5g, of which sugars 2.4g; Fat 46.4g, of which saturates 24.8g; Cholesterol 248mg; Calcium 73mg; Fibre 0.5g; Sodium 205mg.

Dill sauce for **haddock**

The aromatic herb dill is used here to lift the simple cream sauce that accompanies the moist fillets of poached haddock. It gives a tangy piquancy to grilled or poached fish dishes.

SERVES 4

25g/1oz/2 tbsp butter
4 haddock fillets, about 185g/6½oz each
200ml/7fl oz/scant 1 cup milk
200ml/7fl oz/scant 1 cup fish stock
3–4 bay leaves
salt and ground black pepper

FOR THE SAUCE

25g/1oz/2 tbsp butter
75ml/5 tbsp plain (all-purpose) flour
150ml/¼ pint/⅔ cup double (heavy) cream
30–45ml/2–3 tbsp fresh dill
1 egg yolk
dill fronds and slices of lemon, to garnish

1 Melt the butter in a frying pan, then add the haddock fillets, milk, fish stock, bay leaves, and salt and pepper. Bring to a simmer, then poach the fish gently over low heat for 10–15 minutes until tender.

2 To make the sauce, melt the butter in a small pan, add the flour and cook, stirring, for 2 minutes. Remove the pan from the heat and slowly add the double cream, whisking constantly.

3 Chop the dill and stir into the pan with the egg yolk, then return to the heat and simmer for 4 minutes, or until the sauce has thickened. Do not allow the sauce to boil. Season to taste with salt and pepper.

4 Place the haddock fillets on serving plates and pour over the hot sauce. Garnish the fish with dill fronds and slices of lemon, if you like, and serve.

Nutritional information per portion: Energy 503kcal/2097kJ; Protein 36.6g; Carbohydrate 15.5g, of which sugars 1.2g; Fat 33.2g, of which saturates 19.6g; Cholesterol 191mg; Calcium 92mg; Fibre 1g; Sodium 207mg.

Cheese sauce for haddock

This sauce makes fish and vegetable gratins taste delicious. For a thicker coating sauce, increase the amount of flour to 50g/2oz/½ cup and the butter to 50g/2oz/¼ cup.

SERVES 4

1kg/2¼lb haddock fillets
300ml/½ pint/1¼ cups milk
1 small onion, thinly sliced
2 bay leaves
a few black peppercorns

FOR THE SAUCE
25g/1oz/2 tbsp butter
25g/1oz/2 tbsp flour
5ml/1 tsp English (hot) mustard
115g/4oz mature (sharp) hard cheese such as Cheddar, grated
salt and ground black pepper

1 Put the fish in a large pan. Add the milk, onion, bay leaves and peppercorns. Cover and simmer gently for 5–8 minutes, until the fish is just cooked. Lift out with a slotted spoon, straining and reserving the cooking liquid. Flake the fish, removing any bones.

2 To make the sauce, melt the butter in a pan, stir in the flour and cook gently, stirring all the time, for about 1 minute (do not allow it to brown). Remove from the heat and gradually stir in the strained milk.

3 Return to the heat, stirring, until the sauce thickens and comes to the boil. Stir in the mustard and three-quarters of the cheese and season to taste.

4 Stir the fish into the sauce and spoon into individual flameproof dishes. Sprinkle the remaining cheese over the top, and grill (broil) until golden.

Nutritional information per portion: Energy 430kcal/1809kJ; Protein 58.2g; Carbohydrate 9.6g, of which sugars 4.5g; Fat 17.4g, of which saturates 10.6g; Cholesterol 136mg; Calcium 351mg; Fibre 0.4g; Sodium 446mg

Fennel butter sauce for haddock

Fresh fish tastes fabulous cooked in a simple herb butter. Here the fennel complements the haddock beautifully to make a simple dish ideal for a dinner party. If you can buy only small haddock fillets, fold them in half before baking, or use cod as an alternative.

SERVES 4

15g/¼oz butter
675g/1½ lb haddock fillet, skinned and cut into 4 portions
juice of 1 lemon
1 lemon, cut into wafer-thin slices, reserving juice from the lemon

FOR THE SAUCE
40g/1½oz butter
45ml/3 tbsp coarsely chopped fennel
salt and ground black pepper

1 Preheat the oven to 220°C/425°F/Gas 7. Season the fish. Melt the butter in a frying pan and cook the fish. Then transfer the cooked fish to an ovenproof dish.

2 Squeeze the lemon juice over the fish and place the lemon slices on top. Bake for 15–20 minutes, or until the fish is cooked.

3 To make the fennel butter sauce, melt the butter in the frying pan and add the chopped fennel and a little seasoning.

4 Transfer the cooked fish to plates and pour the cooking juices into the herb butter. Heat gently for a few seconds, then pour the herb butter over the fish. Serve immediately.

Nutritional information per portion: Energy 549kcal/2284kJ; Protein 27.9g; Carbohydrate 10.3g, of which sugars 0.9g; Fat 40.9g, of which saturates 5.8g; Cholesterol 60mg; Calcium 341mg; Fibre 0.9g; Sodium 416mg.

Lemon butter sauce for halibut

Some fish have such delicate flavour it is a pity to mask it with heavy sauces. In this elegant dish the sauce is spread on to the steaks with lots of parsley, lemon and butter before cooking, which ensures the flesh is kept succulent and moist.

SERVES 4

4 halibut steaks, about 185g/6½oz each
salt and ground black pepper
parsley sprigs, to garnish (optional)
lemon wedges, to serve

FOR THE SAUCE
150g/5oz/10 tbsp butter, softened
30ml/2 tbsp chopped fresh parsley
30ml/2 tbsp lemon juice

1 Preheat the grill (broiler) to medium. Season the fish with salt and pepper on both sides.

2 To make the sauce, mix together the butter, chopped parsley and lemon juice in a small bowl. Then spread the sauce over the raw fish.

3 Line a grill pan with foil, then put the steaks on the foil. Grill the steaks for about 7–8 minutes on each side, until tender.

4 Serve with lemon wedges for squeezing over, and garnished with parsley sprigs if using.

Nutritional information per portion: Energy 464kcal/1928kJ; Protein 38.2g; Carbohydrate 0.6g, of which sugars 0.5g; Fat 34.3g, of which saturates 20.1g; Cholesterol 141mg; Calcium 83mg; Fibre 0.6g; Sodium 337mg.

Sauce vierge for grilled halibut

Any thick white fish fillets can be used in this versatile dish such as turbot, brill and John Dory. This classic French sauce is heavenly and can be served hot or cold.

SERVES 4

2.5ml/½ tsp fennel seeds
2.5ml/½ tsp celery seeds
5ml/1 tsp mixed peppercorns
5ml/1 tsp fresh thyme leaves, chopped
5ml/1 tsp fresh rosemary leaves, chopped
5ml/1 tsp fresh oregano or marjoram leaves, chopped
105ml/7 tbsp olive oil
675–800g/1½–1⅔lb middle cut of halibut, about 3cm/1½in thick, cut into 4 pieces
coarse sea salt

FOR THE SAUCE

105ml/7 tbsp extra virgin olive oil, plus extra for cooking
juice of 1 lemon
1 garlic clove, finely chopped
2 tomatoes, peeled, seeded and diced
5ml/1 tsp small capers
2 drained canned anchovy fillets, chopped
5ml/1 tsp chopped fresh chives
15ml/1 tbsp shredded fresh basil leaves
15ml/1 tbsp chopped fresh chervil

1 Mix the fennel and celery seeds with the peppercorns in a mortar. Crush with a pestle, and then stir in the coarse sea salt to taste. Spoon the mixture into a shallow dish and stir in the herbs and the olive oil.

2 Heat a ridged griddle pan or preheat the grill (broiler) on high. Brush the griddle pan or grill pan with olive oil to prevent the fish from sticking.

3 Add the halibut pieces to the olive oil mixture, turning to coat them thoroughly, then arrange them with the dark skin uppermost in the oiled griddle pan or grill pan. Cook for about 6–8 minutes, turning once, until the fish is cooked all the way through and the skin has browned.

4 To make the sauce, combine the sauce ingredients, except the fresh herbs, in a pan and heat gently until warm but not hot. Then stir in the chives, basil and chervil.

5 Place the halibut on four warmed plates. Spoon the sauce around and over the fish and serve immediately, with lightly cooked green cabbage, if you like.

Nutritional information per portion: Energy 549kcal/2284kJ; Protein 27.9g; Carbohydrate 10.3g, of which sugars 0.9g; Fat 40.9g, of which saturates 5.8g; Cholesterol 60mg; Calcium 341mg; Fibre 0.9g; Sodium 416mg.

Lemon grass and **chive butter** for **grilled sole**

Chives are at their best when barely cooked, and they make a delicious butter when combined with fragrant lemon grass. Serve with simple grilled fish accompanied by steamed vegetables.

SERVES 4

4 soles, skinned
salt and ground black pepper
a little melted butter, for brushing
lemon or lime wedges, to serve

FOR THE SAUCE

115g/4oz/½ cup unsalted (sweet) butter
5ml/1 tsp chopped lemon grass
pinch of finely grated lime rind
1 kaffir lime leaf, very finely shredded (optional)
45ml/3 tbsp chopped chives or chopped chive flowers, plus extra chives or chive flowers to garnish
2.5–5ml/½–1 tsp Thai fish sauce

1 Cream the butter with the lemon grass, lime rind, lime leaf, if using, and chives or chive flowers. Add the Thai fish sauce, and season to taste.

2 Chill the butter mixture for a short while until it becomes firm enough to handle, then shape it into a roll and wrap in baking parchment. Chill in the refrigerator until firm. Preheat the grill (broiler).

3 Brush the fish with a little melted butter. Place it on the grill rack and season with salt and pepper. Grill (broil) for about 5 minutes on each side, until firm and just cooked.

4 Meanwhile, cut the chilled butter into thin slices. Serve the fish topped with slices of the butter and garnished with chives. Offer lemon or lime wedges with the fish.

Nutritional information per portion: Energy 307kcal/1269kJ; Protein 18.6g; Carbohydrate 0.5g, of which sugars 0.4g; Fat 25.6g, of which saturates 15g; Cholesterol 111mg; Calcium 57mg; Fibre 0.6g; Sodium 278mg.

Red pepper sauce for hake

This version of the French classic steak au poivre is served with a delightfully tangy red pepper relish. It can be made with monkfish or cod instead of the hake.

SERVES 4

30–45ml/2–3 tbsp mixed peppercorns (black, white, pink and green)
4 hake steaks, about 175g/6oz each
30ml/2 tbsp olive oil

FOR THE SAUCE
15ml/1 tbsp olive oil
2 red (bell) peppers, sliced into strips
2 garlic cloves, chopped
4 ripe tomatoes, peeled, seeded and quartered
4 drained canned anchovy fillets, chopped
5ml/1 tsp capers
15ml/1 tbsp balsamic vinegar
12 fresh basil leaves, shredded, plus a few extra to garnish, optional
salt and ground black pepper

1 Put the peppercorns in a mortar and crush them coarsely with a pestle. Season the hake fillets lightly with salt, then coat them evenly on both sides with the crushed peppercorns. Set the coated fish steaks aside.

2 To make the sauce, heat the olive oil in a pan that has a lid. Add the sliced red peppers and stir-fry them for about 5 minutes, until they have slightly softened. Stir in the chopped garlic, tomatoes and the anchovies.

3 Cover the pan and simmer gently for about 20 minutes, until the peppers are very soft. Transfer the contents of the pan into a food processor and process to a coarse purée. Transfer to a bowl and season. Stir in the capers, balsamic vinegar and basil.

4 Heat the olive oil in a pan, and cook the hake for 5 minutes on each side. Place on individual plates with the red pepper sauce. Garnish with basil leaves and balsamic vinegar.

Nutritional information per portion: Energy 283kcal/1186kJ; Protein 33.7g; Carbohydrate 8.2g, of which sugars 8g; Fat 13g, of which saturates 1.9g; Cholesterol 42mg; Calcium 47mg; Fibre 2.3g; Sodium 304mg.

Sweet chilli sauce for **red snapper**

This colourful and sweet-tasting dish combines aromatic bay leaves and olives with fresh green chillies in a rich and spicy tomato sauce that is terrific served with freshly baked fish.

SERVES 4

4 red snappers, cleaned
juice of 2 limes
4 garlic cloves, crushed
5ml/1 tsp dried oregano
2.5ml/½ tsp salt
drained bottled capers, to garnish
lime rind and wedges, to garnish

FOR THE SAUCE

120ml/4fl oz/½ cup olive oil
2 bay leaves
2 garlic cloves, sliced
4 fresh green chillies, seeded and cut in strips
1 onion, thinly sliced
450g/1lb fresh tomatoes
75g/3oz/½ cup pickled jalapeño chilli slices
15ml/1 tbsp soft dark brown sugar
2.5ml/½ tsp ground cloves
2.5ml/½ tsp ground cinnamon
150g/5oz/1¼ cups green olives stuffed with pimiento

1 Preheat the oven to 180°C/350°F/Gas 4. Rinse the fish inside and out. Pat dry with kitchen paper. Place in a large roasting pan in a single layer.

2 Mix the lime juice, garlic, oregano and salt. Pour the mixture evenly all over the fish. Bake for about 30 minutes, or until the flesh flakes easily.

3 To make the sauce, heat the olive oil in a pan, add the bay leaves, sliced garlic and chilli strips. Cook over medium heat, stirring frequently, for 3–4 minutes, until the chilli is softened slightly.

4 Add the onion to the pan and cook for a further 3–4 minutes, stirring often, until the onion is softened and translucent. Keep the heat low and stir the onions often so that they do not brown.

5 Cut a cross in the base of each tomato. Place in a heatproof bowl and pour over boiling water to cover. After 30 seconds, lift the tomatoes out on a slotted spoon and plunge them into a bowl of cold water. Drain. The skins will have begun to peel back.

6 Peel the tomatoes, then cut them in half and squeeze out the seeds. Chop the flesh finely and add it to the onion. Cook for 3–4 minutes, until the tomato begins to soften.

7 Add the pickled jalapeños, brown sugar, ground cloves and cinnamon to the sauce. Cook for about 10 minutes, stirring frequently. Finally, stir in the olives.

8 Pour a little sauce over each fish. Garnish with the capers and lime rind and serve with lime wedges for squeezing over the fish, if you like. Rice goes well with the fish.

Nutritional information per portion: Energy 382kcal/1591kJ; Protein 30.7g; Carbohydrate 8.6g, of which sugars 8.3g; Fat 25.2g, of which saturates 3.9g; Cholesterol 56mg; Calcium 97mg; Fibre 2.4g; Sodium 970mg.

Tomato and lime sauce for swordfish

This fiery tomato sauce is tempered with cooling crème fraîche, making it a wonderful accompaniment to swordfish. The swordfish can be cooked over the barbecue.

SERVES 4

4 swordfish steaks, about 225g/8oz each

FOR THE SAUCE

2 fresh chillies
4 tomatoes
45ml/3 tbsp olive oil
grated rind and juice of 1 lime
2.5ml/½ tsp salt
2.5ml/½ tsp ground black pepper
175ml/6fl oz/¾ cup crème fraîche
fresh flat leaf parsley, to garnish
chargrilled vegetables, to serve

1 Roast the chillies in a pan until the skins are blistered. Seal in a plastic bag and leave for 20 minutes. Peel off the skins, discard the seeds and slice.

2 Cut a cross in the bases of the tomatoes. Place in a bowl and pour over boiling water. After 30 seconds, transfer the tomatoes to a bowl of cold water. Drain. Peel the tomatoes, then cut them in half and squeeze out the seeds. Chop the tomato flesh into 1cm/½in pieces.

3 Heat 15ml/1 tbsp of the oil in a small pan and add the strips of chilli, with the lime rind and juice. Cook for 2–3 minutes, then stir in the tomatoes. Cook for 10 minutes, stirring the mixture occasionally, until the tomatoes are pulpy. Just before serving stir in the crème fraîche.

4 Cook the swordfish steaks under a grill (broiler). Place on individual serving plates and pour the sauce on top. Serve with cooked vegetables if you like.

Nutritional information per portion: Energy 502kcal/2089kJ; Protein 42.2g; Carbohydrate 4.2g, of which sugars 4g; Fat 35.3g, of which saturates 15.2g; Cholesterol 142mg; Calcium 42mg; Fibre 1g; Sodium 311mg.

Horseradish sauce for baked cod

A popular and creamy sauce in England, horseradish sauce is traditionally served with roast beef. In this recipe it gives the succulent baked cod plenty of extra flavour.

SERVES 4

4 thick pieces cod fillet or steaks
15ml/1 tbsp lemon juice
25g/1oz/2 tbsp butter
25g/1oz/¼ cup plain (all-purpose) flour, sifted
150ml/¼ pint/⅔ cup milk
150ml/¼ pint/⅔ cup fish stock
salt and ground black pepper
sprigs of flat leaf parsley, to garnish
potato wedges and fried sliced leeks, to serve

FOR THE SAUCE

30ml/2 tbsp tomato purée (paste)
30ml/2 tbsp grated fresh horseradish
150ml/¼ pint/⅔ cup sour cream

1 Preheat the oven to 180°C/350°F/Gas 4. Place the fish in a buttered ovenproof dish in a single layer. Sprinkle with lemon juice.

2 Melt the butter in a pan. Stir in the flour and cook for 3–4 minutes. Whisk the milk and fish stock into the flour mixture. Season. Return to the heat and bring back to the boil, stirring, and simmer for 3 minutes, still stirring. Pour the sauce over the fish and bake for 20–25 minutes, until cooked.

3 To make the horseradish sauce, blend the tomato purée and horseradish with the sour cream in a small pan. Slowly bring the sauce to the boil, stirring to prevent it from sticking to the pan, and then simmer for 1 minute, until thickened. Pour the horseradish sauce into a serving bowl

4 Serve the fish immediately it is cooked, garnished with the parsley sprigs. Serve with the horseradish sauce, potato wedges and fried sliced leeks.

Nutritional information per portion: Energy 319kcal/1334kJ; Protein 35.6g; Carbohydrate 10.5g, of which sugars 5.5g; Fat 15.2g, of which saturates 8.6g; Cholesterol 120mg; Calcium 111mg; Fibre 0.6g; Sodium 261mg.

Red wine sauce for brill

Spicy yet sweet, this red wine sauce is a perfect accompaniment to fish. The robust sauce adds colour and richness to the dish. Turbot, halibut and John Dory are also good cooked this way.

SERVES 4–6

4 brill fillets, about 175–200g/6–7 oz each, skinned
115g/4oz shallots, thinly sliced
butter for greasing
salt and ground white pepper
fresh chervil or flat leaf parsley leaves, to garnish

FOR THE SAUCE
200ml/7fl oz/scant 1 cup robust red wine
200ml/7fl oz/scant 1 cup fish stock
150g/5oz/2/3 cup chilled butter, diced

1 Preheat the oven to 180°C/350°F/Gas 4. Season the fish on both sides with salt and pepper.

2 Generously butter a flameproof dish, which is large enough to take all the brill fillets in a single layer without overlapping. Spread the shallots over the base and lay the fish fillets on top.

3 Pour over the red wine and fish stock, cover the dish and bring the liquid to just below boiling point. Transfer to the oven and bake for 6–8 minutes, until the brill is just cooked.

4 Using a fish slice (spatula), carefully lift the fish and shallots on to a serving dish, cover with foil and keep hot.

5 To make the sauce, transfer the cooking liquid to a large pan on the hob (stovetop). Bring the liquid to the boil over a high heat and cook until the liquid has reduced by half.

6 Lower the heat and whisk in the chilled butter, one piece at a time, to make a smooth shiny sauce. Season with salt and white pepper, set aside and keep hot.

7 Divide the shallots among four warmed plates and lay the brill fillets on top. Pour the sauce over and around the fish and garnish with the chervil or flat leaf parsley.

Nutritional information per portion: Energy 511kcal/2123kJ; Protein 35.7g; Carbohydrate 1.3g, of which sugars 1.3g; Fat 36.7g, of which saturates 19.5g; Cholesterol 156mg; Calcium 97mg; Fibre 0.4g; Sodium 454mg.

Sour cream sauce for baked pike

This freshwater fish has lean creamy-white flesh and needs to be kept moist during cooking. Here it is gently baked in a creamy sauce for ultimate indulgence. Serve with sautéed potatoes.

SERVES 4–6

1.3kg/3lb whole pike
1 bay leaf

FOR THE SAUCE
15ml/1 tbsp olive oil
50g/2oz/¼ cup butter
1 onion, chopped
1 garlic clove, chopped
115g/4oz/1½ cups wild mushrooms, thickly sliced
15ml/1 tbsp plain (all-purpose) flour
175ml/6fl oz/¾ cup sour cream
15ml/1 tbsp chopped fresh parsley
salt and ground black pepper

1 Preheat the oven to 190°C/375°F/Gas 5. Clean, skin and fillet the pike, putting the bones and skin into a pan. Pour over just enough cold water to cover and add the bay leaf. Bring to the boil, reduce the heat and gently simmer, uncovered, for 20 minutes. Arrange on a greased ovenproof dish.

2 To make the sauce, heat the oil and half the butter in a frying pan and cook the onion until soft. Add the garlic and mushrooms and cook for 2 more minutes. Strain the fish stock and add 300ml/½ pint/1¼ cups of the stock to the onion and mushroom mixture and simmer for 5 minutes.

3 Blend the flour with the sour cream and pour into the onion and mushroom mixture. Bring to the boil, stirring, and carefully pour over the fish. Cover the dish with foil and bake for 30 minutes, until the fish is tender.

Nutritional information per portion: Energy 310kcal/1299kJ; Protein 40.2g; Carbohydrate 3.1g, of which sugars 1.2g; Fat 15.3g, of which saturates 5.7g; Cholesterol 178mg; Calcium 92mg; Fibre 0.3g; Sodium 158mg.

Spiced orange sauce for salmon

This colourful dish uses an Italian method of poaching fish in an orange sauce, known as all' arancia, so this tasty combination is often associated with the Mediterranean.

SERVES 4

4 salmon fillets, each about 175g/6oz
2 oranges, thinly sliced, to garnish
boiled rice, to serve

FOR THE SAUCE
300ml/½ pint/1¼ cups Rhine wine
300ml/½ pint/1¼ cups orange juice
30ml/2 tbsp finely chopped white onion
10ml/2 tsp grated orange rind
pinch of ground cinnamon, plus extra to garnish
pinch of ground ginger
25g/1oz/2 tbsp butter
salt

1 Pour the wine and orange juice into a pan, add the onion, orange rind, cinnamon and ginger and season with salt. Bring to the boil, then lower the heat, cover and simmer for 10 minutes.

2 Add the salmon to the pan, cover and poach gently for 10 minutes. Using a fish slice or metal slotted spatula, transfer the fish to a dish and keep warm.

3 Bring the cooking liquid back to the boil and cook until thickened and reduced. Season the sauce with salt, stir in the butter and ladle the sauce over the salmon. Garnish the salmon with thin unpeeled orange slices, sprinkled with cinnamon. Serve the salmon dish immediately with boiled rice.

Nutritional information per portion: Energy 347kcal/1445kJ; Protein 21.5g; Carbohydrate 12.8g, of which sugars 12.6g; Fat 18.4g, of which saturates 6.5g; Cholesterol 69mg; Calcium 67mg; Fibre 1.2g; Sodium 112mg.

Hollandaise sauce for poached salmon

The secret of success with this rich butter sauce is patience. Work in the butter slowly and thoroughly to give a thick, glossy texture. Serve with a whole poached fish for an elegant dish.

SERVES 8–10

300ml/1/2 pint/1 1/4 cups dry (hard) cider or white wine
1 large carrot, roughly chopped
2 medium onions, roughly chopped
2 celery sticks, roughly chopped
2 bay leaves
a few black peppercorns
sprig of parsley
sprig of thyme
2–2.5kg/4 1/2–5 1/2lb whole salmon, gutted, washed and dried

FOR THE SAUCE
175g/6oz/3/4 cup unsalted (sweet) butter
5ml/1 tsp sugar
3 egg yolks
10ml/2 tsp cider vinegar or white wine vinegar
10ml/2 tsp lemon juice
salt and ground white pepper

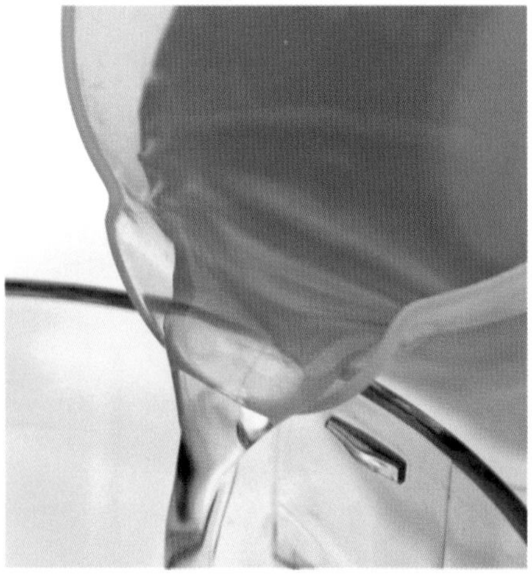

1 Put the cider or white wine, carrot, onions, celery, bay leaves, peppercorns and herbs into a large pan and add 1 litre/1 3/4 pints/4 cups water. Bring to the boil and simmer gently for 30–40 minutes. Strain and leave to cool.

2 About 30 minutes before serving, pour the cooled stock into a fish kettle. Lay the salmon on the rack and lower it into the liquid. Slowly heat the kettle until the stock almost comes to the boil, cover and simmer very gently for 20–25 minutes until the fish is just cooked through.

3 Meanwhile, to make the hollandaise sauce, heat the butter with the sugar (on the stove or in the microwave) until the butter has melted and the mixture is hot but not sizzling – do not allow it to brown.

4 Put the egg yolks, vinegar, lemon juice and seasonings into a processor or blender and blend on high speed for about 15 seconds, or until the mixture is creamy. Then add the hot butter mixture in a slow stream until the sauce is thick, smooth and creamy.

5 Lift the salmon out of its cooking liquid. Remove the skin carefully, so the flesh remains intact, and lift the salmon on to a warmed serving plate. Serve with the warm hollandaise.

Nutritional information per portion: Energy 450kcal/1868kJ; Protein 34.6g; Carbohydrate 0.5g, of which sugars 0.5g; Fat 34.4g, of which saturates 12.8g; Cholesterol 182mg; Calcium 44mg; Fibre 0g; Sodium 183mg.

Cucumber sauce for salmon

The combination of cucumber and fresh dill makes for a refreshing and unusual hot sauce, which really complements the baked salmon. Store the sauce for as short a time as possible.

SERVES 6–8

1.8kg/4lb salmon, cleaned and scaled
melted butter, for brushing
3 fresh parsley or thyme sprigs
1/2 lemon, halved
salt and ground black pepper
orange slices and salad leaves, to serve

FOR THE SAUCE

1 large cucumber, peeled, seeded and diced
25g/1oz/2 tbsp butter
120ml/4fl oz/1/2 cup dry white wine
45ml/3 tbsp finely chopped fresh dill
60ml/4 tbsp sour cream

1 Preheated the oven at 220°C/425°F/Gas 7. Season the salmon and brush with melted butter. Place the herbs and lemon in the cavity. Wrap the salmon securely in foil. Bake in the oven for 15 minutes, then remove from the oven and leave the fish in the foil for 1 hour.

2 To make the sauce, place the cucumber in a colander, toss lightly with salt and leave for 30 minutes.

3 Rinse the cucumber well, drain again and pat dry. Heat the butter in a small pan, add the cucumber and cook for 2 minutes until translucent. Add the wine and boil briskly until the cucumber is dry. Stir in the dill and sour cream and season to taste.

4 Remove the skin from the salmon and fillet. Serve the salmon with the sauce spooned on top, with orange slices and salad leaves, if using.

Nutritional information per portion: Energy 307kcal/1269kJ; Protein 18.6g; Carbohydrate 0.5g, of which sugars 0.4g; Fat 25.6g, of which saturates 15g; Cholesterol 111mg; Calcium 57mg; Fibre 0.6g; Sodium 278mg.

Teriyaki sauce for salmon

Salmon teriyaki is a well-known Japanese dish, which uses a sweet and shiny sauce for marinating as well as for glazing the ingredients. Serve the salmon with sticky rice or soba noodles.

SERVES 4

4 salmon fillets, 150g/5oz each
150ml/¼ pint/⅔ cup sunflower oil
5cm/2in piece of fresh root ginger, peeled and cut into matchsticks

FOR THE SAUCE
45ml/3 tbsp shoyu
45ml/3 tbsp sake
45ml/3 tbsp mirin
15ml/1 tbsp plus 10ml/2 tsp caster (superfine) sugar

1 To make the sauce, mix all the ingredients except 10ml/2 tsp sugar, in a pan. Heat until the sugar has dissolved, then pour into a dish and leave to cool for an hour.

2 Place the fish in the dish with the sauce. Leave for 30 minutes.

3 Heat the oil in a pan and add the ginger. Fry for 1–2 minutes, or until golden and crisp. Remove and drain on kitchen paper.

4 Pour the sauce back into the pan. Add the remaining sugar and heat until dissolved.

5 Heat a griddle pan until smoking hot. Remove the salmon from the marinade and add, skin side down, to the pan. Cook for 2–3 minutes, on each side, or until cooked through.

6 Divide among four serving plates. Top the salmon with the crispy fried ginger. Pour the sauce on top. Serve.

Nutritional information per portion: Energy 337kcal/1408kJ; Protein 31.6g; Carbohydrate 13g, of which sugars 12.5g; Fat 16.6g, of which saturates 2.9g; Cholesterol 75mg; Calcium 49mg; Fibre 0.6g; Sodium 872mg.

Coconut sauce for **salmon**

Salmon is quite a robust fish, and responds well to being cooked with a sauce that is quite pungent, as in this fragrant blend of spices, garlic, chilli and coconut.

SERVES 4

4 salmon steaks, about 175g/6oz each
5ml/1 tsp ground cumin
10ml/2 tsp chilli powder
2.5ml/½ tsp ground turmeric
30ml/2 tbsp white wine vinegar
1.5ml/¼ tsp salt
fresh coriander (cilantro) sprigs, to garnish
rice and sliced spring onions (scallions), to serve

FOR THE SAUCE

45ml/3 tbsp oil
1 onion, chopped
2 fresh green chillies, seeded and chopped
2 garlic cloves, crushed
2.5cm/1in piece fresh root ginger, grated
5ml/1 tsp ground cumin
5ml/1 tsp ground coriander
175ml/6fl oz/¾ cup coconut milk

1 Arrange the salmon steaks in a shallow glass dish. Put the ground cumin in a bowl and add the chilli powder, turmeric, vinegar and salt. Rub the paste over the salmon steaks and leave to marinate for about 15 minutes.

2 To make the sauce, heat the oil in a large frying pan and fry the onion, chillies, garlic and ginger, stirring frequently, for 5–6 minutes, until the onion is softened. Leave to cool slightly.

3 Transfer the onion mixture to a food processor or blender and process to a smooth paste. Return the onion paste to the pan. Add the cumin, the coriander and coconut milk. Bring to the boil, reduce the heat and simmer the sauce for 5 minutes, stirring occasionally.

4 Add the salmon steaks. Cover and cook for 15 minutes, until the fish is tender. Transfer to a serving dish and garnish with the fresh coriander. Serve with the rice and spring onions.

Nutritional information per portion: Energy 416kcal/1729kJ; Protein 36.2g; Carbohydrate 5.2g, of which sugars 4.8g; Fat 27.9g, of which saturates 4.4g; Cholesterol 88mg; Calcium 75mg; Fibre 1.1g; Sodium 132mg.

Whisky cream for salmon

This dish combines two of the finest ingredients of Scotland – salmon and whisky. Although fresh thyme works well in this sauce, you can replace it with whatever fresh herbs are available.

SERVES 4

4 thin pieces salmon fillet, about 175g/6oz each
5ml/1 tsp chopped fresh thyme leaves
50g/2oz/¼ cup butter
salt and ground black pepper
fresh dill sprigs, to garnish

FOR THE SAUCE
75ml/5 tbsp whisky
150ml/¼ pint/⅔ cup double (heavy) cream
juice of ½ lemon (optional)

1 Season the salmon and sprinkle with the thyme. Melt half the butter in a frying pan. When the butter is foaming, fry half the salmon for 2–3 minutes on each side, until they are golden on the outside and just cooked through.

2 Pour in 30ml/2 tbsp of the whisky and ignite it. When the flames have died down, carefully transfer the salmon to a plate and keep it hot. Heat the remaining butter and repeat with the remaining salmon. Keep hot.

3 Pour the cream into the pan and bring to the boil, stirring constantly and scraping the cooking juices off the pan. Simmer until reduced and slightly thickened. Season and add the last of the whisky and a squeeze of lemon if you like.

4 Place the salmon on warmed plates, pour the sauce over and garnish with dill. New potatoes and green beans are good with this.

Nutritional information per portion: Energy 667kcal/2760kJ; Protein 36.1g; Carbohydrate 0.8g, of which sugars 0.8g; Fat 53g, of which saturates 24.5g; Cholesterol 174mg; Calcium 61mg; Fibre 0g; Sodium 164mg.

Avocado, tomato and blue salsa for squid

The use of tomatoes, avocados and a blue cheese takes this delicacy to a different level. For a more aromatic sauce, try adding other fragrant herbs, such as coriander or mint.

SERVES 4

900g/2lb prepared squid
a little olive oil

FOR THE SALSA
2 avocados, peeled, halved and stoned (pitted)
450g/1lb very ripe tomatoes, roughly chopped
2 shallots, chopped
1 red chilli, seeded and finely chopped
15ml/1 tbsp extra virgin olive oil, plus extra for sprinkling
115g/4oz blue cheese, diced
a little lemon juice

1 To make the salsa, cut each avocado half lengthways to make quarters and simply peel off the skin. Cut the fruit into small cubes.

2 Mix the avocado with the tomatoes, shallots and chilli, and combine with the olive oil.

3 Spoon the salsa in mounds on to four individual serving plates.

4 Heat a griddle pan. Brush the squid with olive oil and put straight into the pan, pushing it down gently. After a couple of minutes, turn it over and push down again.

5 When cooked, place the squid on top of the salsa, sprinkle over the diced cheese and then drizzle with a little extra virgin olive oil and lemon juice. Serve immediately.

Nutritional information per portion: Energy 421kcal/1762kJ; Protein 42.2g; Carbohydrate 8.3g, of which sugars 4.6g; Fat 24.5g, of which saturates 8.7g; Cholesterol 527mg; Calcium 181mg; Fibre 3g; Sodium 597mg.

Spicy tomato sauce for prawns

In this dish, prawns are cooked in their shells, in a sticky, spicy sauce. It is best not to use shelled prawns as the shells help to seal in the full flavours of the seafood.

SERVES 4

16 raw tiger prawns (jumbo shrimp)
45ml/3 tbsp vegetable or groundnut (peanut) oil
1 large onion, finely sliced
2 tomatoes, quartered

FOR THE SAUCE

30ml/2 tbsp tomato sauce
15ml/1 tbsp oyster sauce
15ml/1 tbsp plum sauce
15ml/1 tbsp chilli sauce
90ml/6 tbsp water

1 Snip off about 1cm/½in from the head of each prawn, removing the feelers. Wash and pat dry.

2 In a dry wok, fry the prawns over high heat for 3 minutes, until they are nearly cooked. Set aside.

3 Add the oil to the wok and fry the onions until soft. Add the tomatoes and stir-fry for 2 minutes.

4 Mix all the ingredients for the sauce together in a bowl until well blended. Stir the mixture into the cooked onion and tomato mixture.

5 Return the prawns to the wok and stir constantly until well incorporated and bubbling. The prawns should be completely cooked after about 2 minutes. Serve immediately in the sauce.

Nutritional information per portion: Energy 166Kcal/693kJ; Protein 10.2g; Carbohydrate 12.2g, of which sugars 10.4g; Fat 8.9g, of which saturates 1.1g; Cholesterol 98mg; Calcium 63mg; Fibre 1.6g; Sodium 225mg.

Romesco sauce for **grilled prawns**

This sauce, from the Catalan region of Spain, is usually served with fish and shellfish. Its main ingredients are sweet peppers, tomatoes, garlic and toasted almonds.

SERVES 4

24 raw king prawns (shrimp)
30–45ml/2–3 tbsp olive oil
fresh flat leaf parsley, to garnish
lemon wedges, to serve

FOR THE SAUCE
2 tomatoes
60ml/4 tbsp olive oil
1 onion, chopped
4 garlic cloves, chopped
1 canned pimiento, chopped
2.5ml/½ tsp dried chilli flakes or powder
75ml/5 tbsp fish stock
30ml/2 tbsp sherry or white wine
10 blanched almonds
15ml/1 tbsp red wine vinegar
salt

1 To make the sauce, immerse the tomatoes in boiling water for about 30 seconds, remove from the pan, then refresh them under cold water. Peel away the skins and roughly chop the flesh.

2 Heat 30ml/2 tbsp of the oil in a pan, add the onion and 3 of the garlic cloves, and cook until soft. Add the pimiento, tomatoes, chilli, fish stock and sherry or wine. Bring to the boil, reduce the heat, then cover and simmer for 30 minutes. Allow to cool slightly.

3 Meanwhile, toast the almonds under the grill (broiler) until golden. Transfer the almonds to a blender or food processor and grind coarsely. Add the remaining 30ml/2 tbsp of oil, the vinegar and the last garlic clove and process the mixture until it is evenly combined. Carefully add the tomato and pimiento sauce and process until smooth. Season with salt to taste and return to the rinsed pan to keep warm.

4 Remove the heads from the prawns, leaving them otherwise unshelled. With a sharp knife, slit each one down the back and remove the dark vein. Rinse and pat dry on kitchen paper.

5 Toss the prawns in olive oil, then spread out in the grill pan. Grill (broil) for 2–3 minutes on each side, until pink. Arrange on a serving platter, garnish with parsley and serve with lemon wedges and the sauce in a small bowl.

Nutritional information per portion: Energy 416kcal/1732kJ; Protein 32.7g; Carbohydrate 7.1g, of which sugars 6.2g; Fat 28.7g, of which saturates 9.6g; Cholesterol 325mg; Calcium 199mg; Fibre 3.1g; Sodium 307mg.

Spinach salsa for steamed mussels

Mussels are an underused shellfish, and have the advantages of combining well with lots of different ingredients. The colours of this dish work well if you leave the mussels in the half-shell.

SERVES 4

64 mussels, scrubbed and bearded, discarding any that are open and with broken shells
8 ripe tomatoes, blanched and peeled
2 spring onions (scallions), finely chopped
dash of white wine

FOR THE SALSA

120ml/4fl oz/½ cup olive oil
2 garlic cloves, crushed
30ml/2 tbsp chopped fresh coriander (cilantro)
115g/4oz/½ cup butter
4 bunches fresh spinach, washed
salt and ground black pepper

1 Put the mussels in a bowl of fresh slightly salted cold water and leave to soak for at least 30 minutes.

2 Remove the stalks from the spinach. Cut the tomatoes into quarters, remove the seeds and dice.

3 Put the mussels and spring onion into a pan, add the wine and cover. Steam for a few minutes until the shells open and leave to cool. Discard any that remain closed.

4 To make the salsa, place the juices that were used to steam the mussels in a bowl and whisk them together with the oil, then add the tomatoes, garlic and coriander.

5 To assemble, break off one shell and loosen the mussel in the other. Cook the spinach in a frying pan with the butter until just wilting, and season, then stir into the salsa. Arrange the shelled mussels on plates and spoon over the salsa.

Nutritional information per portion: Energy 258kcal/1070kJ; Protein 9g; Carbohydrate 4.6g, of which sugars 4.5g; Fat 22.8g, of which saturates 8.4g; Cholesterol 42mg; Calcium 181mg; Fibre 2.4g; Sodium 244mg.

Tomato sauce for stuffed mussels

This attractive dish is a very tasty way to enjoy fresh mussels. For a vibrant and rich red colour use really ripe plum tomatoes in place of the passata or canned tomatoes.

SERVES 4

1kg/2¼lb live mussels, scrubbed and bearded, discarding any that are open and with broken shells
1 garlic clove
2 eggs, beaten
30ml/2 tbsp chopped fresh parsley
25g/1oz/½ cup soft white breadcrumbs
a small handful of fresh basil, leaves torn into shreds
sea salt and ground black pepper

FOR THE SAUCE
75ml/5 tbsp olive oil
2 garlic cloves, peeled
600ml/1 pint/2½ cups passata (bottled strained tomatoes), sieved (strained) canned tomatoes or finely chopped plum tomatoes

1 Cook the mussels in a pan for about 6 minutes. Discard any that remain closed. Drain, reserving any liquid from the mussels.

2 To make the sauce, heat the oil in a pan. Add the garlic cloves to the oil and fry until brown, then lift the cloves out and discard them.

3 Stir the passata or tomatoes into the garlic-flavoured oil and season. Bring to the boil, then lower the heat, cover the pan and simmer the mixture for 20 minutes.

4 Meanwhile, make the stuffing. Chop the garlic clove and put it in a bowl. Add the eggs, parsley and breadcrumbs. Season to taste with salt and pepper. Then fill the empty half shell of each mussel with the stuffing, then tie each one with string (twine).

5 Add the reserved liquid from the mussels to the tomato sauce, with the basil. Stir to mix, then add the mussels. Cover the pan tightly and simmer for 10 minutes. Remove the string. Serve immediately.

Nutritional information per portion: Energy 366kcal/1537kJ; Protein 21.2g; Carbohydrate 29g, of which sugars 6.5g; Fat 19.3g, of which saturates 3.1g; Cholesterol 125mg; Calcium 238mg; Fibre 3g; Sodium 441mg.

Garlic and white wine sauce for mussels

This recipe is the simplest way to serve these delicious seafood morsels. Unlike many other European mussel recipes, the sauce is thickened with breadcrumbs before serving.

SERVES 4

2kg/4½lb mussels

FOR THE SAUCE
45ml/3 tbsp olive oil
200ml/7fl oz/scant 1 cup white wine
2 garlic cloves, chopped
bunch of fresh parsley, trimmed and chopped
about 50g/2oz/1 cup fresh white breadcrumbs
ground black pepper

1 Gently scrub the mussels, scraping off any barnacles and pulling out the fibrous 'beards' that are used by the creatures to cling on to rocks. Discard any open mussels that do not shut when lightly tapped.

2 To make the sauce, pour the olive oil and wine into a large pan. Add the garlic and parsley and season with a little pepper, but do not add salt.

3 Bring to the boil, add the mussels, then cover with a tight-fitting lid and cook over medium heat, shaking the pan occasionally, for 4–5 minutes, or until the mussels have all opened up.

4 Use a slotted spoon to remove the mussels (discarding any mussels that do not open) and place in a large bowl. Strain the cooking liquid through a sieve (strainer) lined with muslin (cheesecloth) and return to the rinsed-out pan.

5 Add the breadcrumbs to the sauce and bring to the boil, stirring frequently. Boil for about a minute so that the breadcrumbs thicken the sauce.

6 Add a little more wine and/or breadcrumbs, if necessary, to give the sauce a good consistency. Boil again after adding any additional wine or crumbs.

7 Divide the mussels between warmed serving dishes. Return any juices from the bowl to the sauce and then pour it over them. Serve immediately. This dish is delicious served with a fine white wine such as a Chenin Blanc, Pinot Blanc or Pinot Grigio.

Nutritional information per portion: Energy 549kcal/2284kJ; Protein 27.9g; Carbohydrate 10.3g, of which sugars 0.9g; Fat 40.9g, of which saturates 5.8g; Cholesterol 60mg; Calcium 341mg; Fibre 0.9g; Sodium 416mg.

Beurre noisette for **scallops**

This dish combines bacon and scallops with brown butter which has just begun to burn but not quite. It gives a lovely nutty smell, which is why the French call this dish 'noisette' – nutty.

SERVES 4

12 rashers (strips) streaky (fatty) bacon
12 scallops
30ml/2 tbsp chopped fresh flat leaf parsley

FOR THE SAUCE

225g/8oz/1 cup unsalted (sweet) butter, cut into chunks
juice of 1 lemon

1 Preheat the grill (broiler) to high. Wrap a rasher of bacon around each scallop so it goes over the top and not round the side.

2 Grill (broil) the scallops with the bacon facing up so it protects the meat. The bacon fat will help to cook the scallops. This will take only a few minutes; once they are cooked set aside and keep warm.

3 Put the butter into a small pan over low heat. Allow to turn a nutty brown colour, gently swirling it. Just as it is foaming, take off the heat and add the lemon juice. It will bubble up quite dramatically.

4 Place the scallops on warmed plates, dress with plenty of chopped fresh parsley and pour the butter sauce over.

Nutritional information per portion: Energy 665kcal/2749kJ; Protein 24.4g; Carbohydrate 2.7g, of which sugars 0.6g; Fat 62g, of which saturates 34.7g; Cholesterol 189mg; Calcium 51mg; Fibre 0.5g; Sodium 1240mg.

Black bean sauce for scallops

Sweet tender flesh of the scallops is perfectly complemented with a little flavoursome sauce made from Chinese wine, black bean sauce and fresh ginger.

SERVES 4

8 scallops, preferably in the shell
15ml/1 tbsp spring onions (scallions), chopped, to garnish

FOR THE SAUCE

30ml/2 tbsp Chinese Hsiao Hsing wine
15ml/1 tbsp fermented black beans
15ml/1 tbsp chopped fresh root ginger
2.5ml/1/2 tsp sugar

1 Preheat the oven to 160°C/325°F/Gas 3. Spread the scallops on a baking sheet. Heat until they gape. Remove them from the oven.

2 Using a knife, run the blade along the inner surface of the flat shell to cut through the muscle that holds the shells together.

3 Ease the shells apart. Lift off the top shell. Pull out and discard the black intestinal sac and the yellowish frilly membrane.

4 Cut the white scallop and orange coral from the shell and rinse briefly under cold water. Remove and discard the white ligament attached to the scallop flesh.

5 To make the sauce, mix the wine, black beans, ginger and sugar in a shallow dish. Add the scallops and marinate for 30 minutes.

6 Return the scallops and sauce to the shells and steam for 10 minutes. Garnish with spring onions. Serve.

Nutritional information per portion: Energy 75kcal/319kJ; Protein 12.3g; Carbohydrate 3.9g, of which sugars 0.9g; Fat 0.8g, of which saturates 0.2g; Cholesterol 24mg; Calcium 19mg; Fibre 0.3g; Sodium 91mg.

Chilli and yellow bean sauce for clams

Yellow bean sauce has a lovely, nutty tang that blends well with most ingredients, especially seafood. This Thai-inspired dish is very easy to prepare and can be made in a matter of minutes.

SERVES 4–6

1kg/2¼ lb fresh clams, washed and scrubbed
handful of basil leaves, plus extra to garnish
3 red chillies, seeded and chopped, to garnish

FOR THE SAUCE
30ml/2 tbsp vegetable oil
4 garlic cloves, finely chopped
15ml/1 tbsp grated fresh root ginger
4 shallots, finely chopped
30ml/2 tbsp yellow bean sauce
3 red chillies, seeded and chopped
15ml/1 tbsp fish sauce
pinch of sugar

1 To make the sauce, heat the vegetable oil in a wok or large frying pan. Add the garlic and ginger and fry for about 30 seconds. Then add the shallots to the pan and fry for a further minute.

2 Next add the washed clams to the pan. Using a fish slice or spatula, turn them a few times so the clams are well coated all over with the oil. Add the yellow bean sauce and the chopped red chillies.

3 Continue to cook, stirring often, for 5–7 minutes, or until all the clams are open. You may need to add a splash of water.

4 Add the fish sauce and a little sugar to sweeten the sauce.

5 Check and adjust the seasoning, adding more fish sauce if needed. Finally add the basil leaves and stir to mix.

6 Transfer the clams to a serving platter. Garnish with the chopped red chillies and basil leaves and pour over the sauce. Serve immediately.

Nutritional information per portion: Energy 94kcal/393kJ; Protein 11.6g; Carbohydrate 2.4g, of which sugars 0.6g; Fat 4.3g, of which saturates 0.6g; Cholesterol 45mg; Calcium 75mg; Fibre 0.7g; Sodium 998mg.

Curry sauce for crab

This mild yellow curry sauce can be served with seafood, meat or chicken. The distinctive flavour and aroma is achieved by a blend of curry powder, ginger, lime juice and coconut milk.

SERVES 4

8 mottled blue crabs
boiled rice, to serve

FOR THE SAUCE
1/2 large onion, chopped
5 garlic cloves, chopped
15ml/1 tbsp grated fresh root ginger
30ml/2 tbsp seafood curry powder, blended with a little water to make a paste
60ml/4 tbsp oil
475ml/16fl oz/2 cups coconut milk
30ml/2 tbsp lime juice
5ml/1 tsp salt

1 Remove the shells of the crabs and discard the spongy fibrous tissues.

2 Separate the claws from the bodies if they are large. The smaller legs have very little meat in them, but leave them attached to the bodies as they make good handles for eating with the fingers.

3 Grind the onion, garlic cloves and ginger together using a mortar and pestle or a food processor to make a paste. Mix the curry powder, blended with water, into the mixture.

4 Heat the oil in a wok or large pan and fry the spice paste for 3 minutes. Add the coconut milk, lime juice and salt and simmer for 2 minutes.

5 Add the crabs to the sauce and cook for about 8 minutes, turning constantly, until the shells have turned completely pink. Serve with rice.

Nutritional information per portion: Energy 288Kcal/1205kJ; Protein 22.5g; Carbohydrate 11.6g, of which sugars 7.1g; Fat 17.4g, of which saturates 2.2g; Cholesterol 55mg; Calcium 86mg; Fibre 0.6g; Sodium 506mg.

Thermidor sauce for lobster

One of the classic French dishes, Lobster Thermidor makes a little lobster go a long way. It is best to use one big rather than two small lobsters, as a larger lobster will contain sweeter meat.

SERVES 2

1 large lobster, about 800g–1kg/ 1¾–2¼lb, boiled, halved lengthways
45ml/3 tbsp brandy

FOR THE SAUCE
25g/1oz/2 tbsp butter
2 shallots, finely chopped
115g/4oz/1½ cups button (white) mushrooms, thinly sliced
15ml/1 tbsp plain (all-purpose) flour
105ml/7 tbsp fish or shellfish stock
120ml/4fl oz/½ cup double (heavy) cream
5ml/1 tsp Dijon mustard
2 egg yolks, beaten
45ml/3 tbsp dry white wine
45ml/3 tbsp freshly grated Parmesan
salt, ground black pepper and cayenne pepper

1 Crack the lobster claws. Discard the stomach sac. Keeping each half-shell intact, extract the meat, then dice. Place in a dish and add the brandy.

2 To make the sauce, melt the butter in a pan and cook the shallots over low heat until soft. Add the mushrooms and cook until tender, stirring constantly. Stir in the flour and a pinch of cayenne; cook, stirring, for 2 minutes. Gradually add the stock, stirring until the sauce boils and thickens.

3 Stir in the cream and mustard and continue to cook until smooth and thick. Season to taste with salt, black pepper and cayenne. Pour half the sauce on to the egg yolks, stir well and return the mixture to the pan. Stir in the wine; adjust the seasoning, being generous with the cayenne.

4 Stir the diced lobster and the brandy into the sauce. Arrange the lobster half-shells in a grill pan (broiler) and divide the mixture among them. Sprinkle with Parmesan and place under the grill until browned. Serve immediately.

Nutritional information per portion: Energy 859kcal/3573kJ; Protein 56g; Carbohydrate 9.8g, of which sugars 2g; Fat 59.6g, of which saturates 33.8g; Cholesterol 536mg; Calcium 488mg; Fibre 1.2g; Sodium 976mg.

Sauces for poultry, meat and game

This section includes creative combinations based on flavours from around the world. The sauces are partnered with specific main ingredients in these recipes so that they can be prepared as part of a complete meal – whether 'cooking in' or 'pouring on'. There are rich long-simmered sauces, fruity ones, and lightly-spiced sauces.

Bread sauce and **Madeira gravy** for **chicken**

Smooth and surprisingly delicate, this old-fashioned sauce is traditionally served with a succulent roast chicken and makes a perfect family meal. For a lighter spiced sauce, reduce the number of cloves and add a little freshly grated nutmeg instead.

SERVES 4

50g/2oz/¼ cup butter
1 onion, chopped
75g/3oz/1½ cups fresh white breadcrumbs
grated rind of 1 lemon
30ml/2 tbsp chopped fresh parsley
30ml/2 tbsp chopped fresh tarragon
1 egg yolk
1.5kg/3¼lb oven-ready chicken
175g/6oz rindless streaky (fatty) bacon rashers (strips)
salt and ground black pepper

FOR THE SAUCE
1 onion, studded with 6 cloves
1 bay leaf
300ml/½ pint/1¼ cups milk
150ml/¼ pint/⅔ cup single (light) cream
115g/4oz/2 cups fresh white breadcrumbs
knob (pat) of butter

FOR THE GRAVY
10ml/2 tsp plain (all-purpose) flour
300ml/½ pint/1¼ cups chicken stock
dash of Madeira or sherry

1 Preheat the oven to 200°C/400°F/Gas 6. First make the stuffing. Melt half the butter in a pan and cook the onion for about 5 minutes, or until softened but not coloured.

2 Remove the pan from the heat and add the breadcrumbs, lemon rind, parsley and half the chopped tarragon. Season, then mix in the egg yolk to bind the ingredients into a moist stuffing.

3 Fill the neck end of the chicken with stuffing, then truss the chicken neatly and weigh it. To calculate the cooking time, allow 20 minutes per 450g/1lb, plus an extra 20 minutes. Put the chicken in a roasting pan and season it well with salt and pepper. Beat together the remaining butter and tarragon, then smear this over the bird.

4 Lay the bacon rashers over the chicken (this helps stop the meat from drying out) and roast for the calculated time. Baste the bird every 30 minutes during cooking and cover with buttered foil if the bacon begins to overbrown.

5 Meanwhile, make the bread sauce. Put the clove-studded onion, bay leaf and milk in a small, heavy pan and bring to the boil over low heat. Remove the pan from the heat and leave the milk to stand for at least 30 minutes so that it is infused (steeped) with the flavourings.

6 Strain the milk into a clean pan (discard the flavouring ingredients) and add the cream and breadcrumbs. Bring slowly to the boil, stirring constantly, then reduce the heat and simmer gently for 5 minutes. Keep warm while you make the gravy and carve the chicken, then stir in the butter and season to taste just before serving.

7 Transfer the cooked chicken to a large pre-warmed serving dish, and cover tightly with foil. Leave the chicken to stand for 10 minutes.

8 To make the gravy, pour off all but 15ml/1 tbsp fat from the roasting pan. Place the pan on the stove and stir in the flour. Cook for about 1 minute, until golden brown, then gradually stir in the stock and Madeira or sherry. Bring to the boil, stirring, then simmer for about 3 minutes, until thickened. Add seasoning to taste and strain the gravy into a warm sauce boat.

9 Carve the chicken and serve it immediately, with the stuffing, gravy and hot bread sauce.

Nutritional information per portion: Energy 673kcal/2814kJ; Protein 41.8g; Carbohydrate 46.3g, of which sugars 7.9g; Fat 35.4g, of which saturates 13.3g; Cholesterol 246mg; Calcium 215mg; Fibre 1.7g; Sodium 537mg.

Coronation sauce for chicken

Originally devised as part of the feast to celebrate the coronation of Elizabeth II in 1953, this traditional and delightfully tasty sauce has inspired chefs ever since.

SERVES 8

2.25kg/5lb chicken, cooked
juice of 1/2 lemon
watercress sprigs, to garnish

FOR THE SAUCE
1 small onion, chopped
15g/1/2oz/1 tbsp butter
15ml/1 tbsp curry paste
15ml/1 tbsp tomato paste
120ml/4fl oz/1/2 cup red wine
1 bay leaf
juice of 1/2 lemon, or to taste
10–15ml/2–3 tsp apricot jam
300ml/1/2 pint/1 1/4 cups mayonnaise
120ml/4fl oz/1/2 cup whipping cream
salt and ground black pepper

1 Remove all the skin and bones from the cooked chicken and chop the flesh into pieces.

2 To make the sauce, cook the chopped onion in the butter until soft. Add the curry paste, tomato paste, wine, bay leaf and lemon juice, then continue to cook gently for about 10 minutes.

3 Add the apricot jam to the pan and stir into the sauce, then press through a sieve (strainer) and cool. Then beat the sauce into the mayonnaise.

4 Whip the cream and fold it in; add seasoning and lemon juice to taste. Stir in the chicken. Garnish with watercress and serve.

Nutritional information per portion: Energy 587kcal/2429kJ; Protein 10.1g; Carbohydrate 17.1g, of which sugars 4.7g; Fat 51.6g, of which saturates 8.8g; Cholesterol 228mg; Calcium 97mg; Fibre 1.1g; Sodium 401mg.

Tarragon and parsley sauce for chicken

The aniseed-like flavour of tarragon has a particular affinity with chicken, especially in creamy sauces. Serve seasonal vegetables and boiled rice with the chicken.

SERVES 4

30ml/2 tbsp light olive oil
4 chicken breast portions (about 250g/9oz each), skinned
sprigs of fresh tarragon and flat leaf parsley, to garnish

FOR THE SAUCE

3 shallots, finely chopped
2 garlic cloves, finely chopped
115g/4oz/1½ cups wild mushrooms (such as chanterelles or ceps) or shiitake mushrooms, halved
150ml/¼ pint/⅔ cup dry white wine
300ml/½ pint/1¼ cups double (heavy) cream
15g/½oz/¼ cup chopped mixed fresh tarragon and flat leaf parsley
salt and ground black pepper

1 Heat the olive oil in a frying pan and add the chicken, skin side down. Cook for 10 minutes, turning the chicken until it is a golden brown colour on both sides.

2 Reduce the heat and cook the chicken for 10 minutes more, turning occasionally. Remove from the pan and set aside.

3 To make the sauce, add the shallots and garlic to the pan and cook gently, stirring, until the shallots are soft but not brown.

4 Increase the heat, add the mushrooms and stir-fry for about 2 minutes. Replace the chicken, then pour in the wine. Simmer for 5–10 minutes, or until most of the wine has evaporated.

5 Add the cream and gently mix the ingredients together. Simmer for 10 minutes, or until the sauce has thickened. Stir the herbs into the sauce and season to taste. Arrange the chicken on warm plates and spoon the sauce over. Garnish with tarragon and parsley.

Nutritional information per portion: Energy 722kcal/3003kJ; Protein 62.1g; Carbohydrate 2.9g, of which sugars 2.5g; Fat 48.8g, of which saturates 26.6g; Cholesterol 278mg; Calcium 66mg; Fibre 0.7g; Sodium 171mg.

Lemon sauce for chicken

Succulent chicken with a refreshing lemony sauce is a sure winner. The Chinese-style sauce is also excellent with steamed white fish, marinated in sesame oil and sherry before cooking.

SERVES 4

4 small chicken breast fillets, skinned
5ml/1 tsp sesame oil
15ml/1 tbsp dry sherry
1 egg white, lightly beaten
30ml/2 tbsp cornflour (cornstarch)
15ml/1 tbsp vegetable oil
salt and ground white pepper
chopped coriander (cilantro) leaves, spring onions (scallions) and lemon wedges, to garnish

FOR THE SAUCE
45ml/3 tbsp fresh lemon juice
30ml/2 tbsp sweetened lime juice
45ml/3 tbsp caster (superfine) sugar
10ml/2 tsp cornflour
90ml/6 tbsp cold water

1 Place the chicken in a shallow bowl. Mix the sesame oil with the sherry and add 2.5ml/½ tsp salt and 1.5ml/¼ tsp pepper. Pour over the chicken, cover and marinate for 15 minutes.

2 Mix the egg white and cornflour. Add the mixture to the chicken and turn to coat thoroughly. Heat the vegetable oil in a non-stick frying pan or wok and fry the chicken fillets for about 15 minutes, until cooked.

3 Meanwhile, make the sauce. Combine all the ingredients in a small pan. Add 1.5ml/½ tsp salt. Bring to the boil over low heat, stirring constantly until the sauce is smooth and has thickened slightly.

4 Cut the chicken into pieces and arrange on a plate. Pour the sauce over the chicken, garnish with the coriander, spring onions and lemon and serve.

Nutritional information per portion: Energy 282kcal/1194kJ; Protein 36.9g; Carbohydrate 22.3g, of which sugars 14.2g; Fat 5.2g, of which saturates 0.9g; Cholesterol 105mg; Calcium 17mg; Fibre 0g; Sodium 112mg.

Hot chilli salsa for **chicken**

These delicious marinated chicken breasts make a good choice for a light meal. This sweet-sour salsa also goes well with grilled fish. For a milder sauce, discard the chilli seeds.

SERVES 4

30ml/2 tbsp fresh lemon juice
30ml/2 tbsp olive oil
10ml/2 tsp ground cumin
10ml/2 tsp dried oregano
15ml/1 tbsp coarse black pepper
4 chicken breast portions, about 175g/6oz each, boned and skinned

FOR THE SALSA
1 fresh hot green chilli
450g/1lb tomatoes, seeded and chopped
3 spring onions (scallions), chopped
15ml/1 tbsp chopped fresh parsley
30ml/2 tbsp chopped coriander (cilantro)
30ml/2 tbsp fresh lemon juice
45ml/3 tbsp olive oil

1 In a shallow dish, combine the lemon juice, oil, cumin, oregano and pepper. Add the chicken and turn to coat. Cover and leave to stand in a cool place for at least 2 hours, or place in the refrigerator and chill overnight.

2 To make the salsa, char the chilli skin either over a gas flame or under the grill (broiler). Leave to cool for 5 minutes. Wearing rubber gloves, carefully rub off the charred skin from the chillies. Chop the chilli very finely and place in a bowl. Add the tomatoes, spring onions, parsley, coriander, lemon juice and olive oil. Mix well to combine.

3 Remove the chicken from the marinade. Heat a ridged griddle. Add the chicken breasts and cook for about 3 minutes until browned on one side. Turn them over and cook for 3–4 minutes more. Serve with the chilli salsa.

Nutritional information per portion: Energy 430kcal/1809kJ; Protein 58.2g; Carbohydrate 9.6g, of which sugars 4.5g; Fat 17.4g, of which saturates 10.6g; Cholesterol 136mg; Calcium 351mg; Fibre 0.4g; Sodium 446mg.

Egg and lemon sauce for chicken

This recipe of slow-cooked chicken and giblets draws on the contrasting flavours of egg and lemon, with the chopped parsley providing a fresh finish to this simple and enjoyable meal.

SERVES 4–6

200g/7oz chicken giblets
15g/½oz/1 tbsp unsalted (sweet) butter
90ml/6 tbsp extra virgin olive oil
1 oven-ready free-range chicken, about 3kg/6lb 9oz
chicken stock, as needed
sea salt
handful chopped fresh flat leaf parsley and lemon slices, to garnish

FOR THE SAUCE
3 eggs, beaten
juice and grated rind of ½ large, unwaxed lemon

1 Clean and trim all the giblets and chop them coarsely. Put them in a deep pan with a lid over medium heat and add the butter and olive oil. Cook for 5 minutes. Lay the chicken in the pan and cook briefly on all sides to seal.

2 Pour in an even mixture of water and chicken stock to come about three-quarters of the way up the pan. Add salt and cover tightly, then simmer gently for about 1½–2 hours, or until the chicken is cooked through.

3 The liquid in the pan should have almost completely evaporated. Take the chicken out of the pan and carve it into portions. Arrange the carved chicken on a warmed serving dish.

4 To make the sauce, whisk together the beaten eggs and the juice and rind of the lemon, then add the mixture to the juices left in the pan. Beat until the eggs thicken slightly.

5 Pour the sauce over the cooked chicken portions, sprinkle with chopped parsley and serve immediately, garnished with lemon slices, if using.

Nutritional information per portion: Energy 765kcal/3174kJ; Protein 64.1g; Carbohydrate 0g, of which sugars 0g; Fat 56.3g, of which saturates 17.1g; Cholesterol 421mg; Calcium 40mg; Fibre 0g; Sodium 304mg.

Sherry and **tomato sauce** for **chicken**

In this tasty dish, chicken portions are first fried, then smothered in a rich, herby tomato sauce and baked in the oven. It's also good with pan-fried pork or lamb. Serve with rice and basil leaves.

SERVES 8

8 chicken portions
1.5ml/1/4 tsp chopped fresh thyme
40g/1 1/2oz/3 tbsp butter
45ml/3 tbsp vegetable oil
3–4 garlic cloves, crushed
2 onions, finely chopped
salt and ground black pepper
cooked rice, to serve
basil leaves, to garnish

FOR THE SAUCE
120ml/4fl oz/1/2 cup dry sherry
45ml/3 tbsp tomato (purée) paste
a few fresh basil leaves
30ml/2 tbsp white wine vinegar
generous pinch of sugar
5ml/1 tsp French mustard
400g/14oz can chopped tomatoes
225g/8oz/3 cups mushrooms, sliced

1 Preheat the oven to 180°C/350°F/Gas 4. Season the chicken with salt, pepper and thyme. In a frying pan heat the butter and oil, and cook the chicken until golden. Then place in an ovenproof dish and keep hot. Add the garlic and onions to the pan and cook, stirring, for 2–3 minutes, or until soft.

2 To make the sauce, mix together the sherry, tomato paste, salt and pepper, basil, vinegar and sugar. Add the mustard and tomatoes.

3 Pour the sauce mixture into the pan and bring to the boil. Reduce the heat and add the mushrooms. Adjust the seasoning with more sugar or vinegar.

4 Pour the tomato sauce over the chicken. Bake in the oven, covered, for 45–60 minutes, or until the chicken is cooked right through. Serve on a bed of rice, garnished with torn basil leaves, if you like.

Nutritional information per portion: Energy 335kcal/1388kJ; Protein 20g; Carbohydrate 5.7g, of which sugars 4.7g; Fat 24.1g, of which saturates 7.7g; Cholesterol 107mg; Calcium 26mg; Fibre 1.5g; Sodium 127mg.

Marsala cream for turkey

The combination of Marsala and cream makes a very rich and opulent sauce. The addition of lemon juice gives it a refreshing tang, which offsets the richness just perfectly.

SERVES 6

6 turkey breast steaks
45ml/3 tbsp plain (all-purpose) flour
30ml/2 tbsp olive oil
25g/1oz/2 tbsp butter
salt and ground black pepper
lemon wedges and chopped fresh parsley, to garnish
mangetouts (snow peas) and green beans, to serve, (optional)

FOR THE SAUCE

175ml/6fl oz/¾ cup dry Marsala
60ml/4 tbsp lemon juice
175ml/6fl oz/¾ cup double (heavy) cream

1 Put each turkey steak between clear film (plastic wrap) and pound with a rolling pin to flatten out evenly. Cut each steak in half or into quarters.

2 Put the flour in a bowl. Season with salt and pepper and coat the meat.

3 Heat the oil and butter in a frying pan until sizzling. Add the turkey and sauté over medium heat for about 3 minutes on each side until tender. Then transfer to a warmed dish and keep hot.

4 To make the sauce, mix the Marsala and lemon juice in a bowl, add to the oil and butter remaining in the pan. Bring to the boil, then add the cream.

5 Heat gently until simmering, then continue to simmer, stirring constantly, until the sauce is reduced and glossy. Spoon the sauce over the turkey, garnish with the lemon wedges and parsley and serve immediately.

Nutritional information per portion: Energy 391kcal/1625kJ; Protein 29.7g; Carbohydrate 6.8g, of which sugars 1.1g; Fat 23.8g, of which saturates 12.8g; Cholesterol 115mg; Calcium 32mg; Fibre 0.2g; Sodium 93mg.

Plum sauce for duck

Sharp plums partner perfectly with the duck in this updated version of an old English dish. For a spicier sauce, add finely chopped chillies and grated ginger.

SERVES 4

4 duck quarters

FOR THE SAUCE

1 large red onion, finely chopped
500g/1¼ lb ripe plums, stoned (pitted) and quartered
30ml/2 tbsp redcurrant jelly

1 Prick the duck skin all over with a fork to release the fat during cooking and help give a crisp result, then place the portions in a heavy frying pan, skin side down.

2 Cook the duck pieces for about 10 minutes on each side, or until golden brown and cooked right through. Remove the duck from the frying pan using a slotted spoon and keep warm.

3 To make the sauce, pour away all but 30ml/2 tbsp of the duck fat, then stir-fry the onion for 5 minutes, or until golden. Add the plums and cook for a further 5 minutes, stirring frequently. Add the redcurrant jelly and mix well.

4 Replace the duck portions and cook for a further 5 minutes, or until thoroughly reheated. Serve immediately while hot.

Nutritional information per portion: Energy 334kcal/1405kJ; Protein 33g; Carbohydrate 22g, of which sugars 21g; Fat 13g, of which saturates 4g; Cholesterol 144mg; Calcium 48mg; Fibre 2.8g; Sodium 100mg.

Damson and ginger sauce for duck

A celebrated Welsh recipe that would typically consist of sharp-tasting fruit sauce of damsons, plums or whinberries. Both the duck and sauce are also good served cold.

SERVES 4

4 duck breast portions
15ml/1 tbsp oil
salt and ground black pepper

FOR THE SAUCE
250g/9oz fresh damsons
5ml/1 tsp ground ginger
45ml/3 tbsp sugar
10ml/2 tsp wine vinegar or sherry vinegar

1 To make the sauce, put the damsons in a pan with the ginger and 45ml/3 tbsp water. Bring to the boil, cover and simmer for about 5 minutes, or until the fruit is soft. Stir frequently, adding extra water if the fruit looks as if it is drying out.

2 Stir in the sugar and vinegar. Press the mixture through a sieve (strainer) to remove stones (pits) and skin. Taste the sauce and add more sugar if necessary, and season.

3 Meanwhile, score the fat on the duck breast portions without cutting into the meat. Brush the oil over both sides of the duck. Sprinkle salt and pepper on the fat side only.

4 Preheat a pan. Add the duck breast portions, skin side down, and cook over medium heat for 5 minutes. Turn over and cook the meat side for 5 minutes. Lift out and leave to rest for 5–10 minutes. Slice the duck and serve with the sauce.

Nutritional information per portion: Energy 275kcal/1157kJ; Protein 29.9g; Carbohydrate 17.5g, of which sugars 17.5g; Fat 12.5g, of which saturates 2.4g; Cholesterol 165mg; Calcium 39mg; Fibre 1.1g; Sodium 167mg.

Sherried almond sauce for guinea fowl

The Arabs introduced saffron to Spain and this is a lavish sauce of toasted almonds ground with parsley and several spices, flavoured with precious saffron. Serve with crusty bread.

SERVES 4

1.2–1.3kg/2½–3lb guinea fowl

FOR THE SAUCE

25g/1oz/¼ cup blanched almonds
pinch of saffron threads
120ml/4fl oz/½ cup chicken stock
60ml/4 tbsp olive oil
1 thick slice of bread, without crusts
2 garlic cloves, finely chopped
120ml/4fl oz/½ cup sherry
1 bay leaf, crumbled
4 thyme sprigs
15ml/1 tbsp finely chopped fresh parsley
pinch of freshly grated nutmeg
pinch of ground cloves
juice of ½ lemon
5ml/1 tsp paprika
salt and ground black pepper

1 Preheat the oven to 150°C/300°F/Gas 2. Spread the almonds on a baking sheet and toast in the oven for about 20 minutes until golden brown.

2 Crumble the saffron with your fingers into a jug (pitcher) or small bowl, pour over 30ml/2 tbsp hot chicken stock and leave to soak.

3 Cut the bird into eight serving pieces, discarding the wing tips, backbone, breastbones and leg tips. This will give you two legs (split them at the joint), two wings with one-third of the breast attached, and two short breast pieces.

4 Heat the olive oil in a shallow flameproof casserole and fry the bread on both sides. Fry the garlic quickly. Transfer both to a blender.

5 Season the fowl and fry until golden all over. Add the remaining stock and sherry, stirring. Add the bay leaf and thyme. Cover and cook gently for 10 minutes.

6 Grind the bread and garlic with the almonds in a food processor. Add the parsley, saffron liquid, nutmeg and cloves, and process to a purée. Stir the mixture into the sauce with the lemon juice, paprika and season with salt and pepper. Serve the guinea fowl with the sauce poured over.

Nutritional information per portion: Energy 534kcal/2221kJ; Protein 45.8g; Carbohydrate 4.5g, of which sugars 1.1g; Fat 33.4g, of which saturates 8.2g; Cholesterol 345mg; Calcium 92mg; Fibre 1.1g; Sodium 145mg.

Whisky sauce for **guinea fowl**

Guinea fowl is magnificent when served with this rich, creamy whisky sauce. If you don't have whisky, then use brandy, Madeira or Marsala. Or even use freshly squeezed orange juice instead.

SERVES 4

2 guinea fowl, each weighing about 1kg/2¼lb

FOR THE SAUCE

90ml/6 tbsp whisky

150ml/¼ pint/⅔ cup well-flavoured chicken stock

150ml/¼ pint/⅔ cup double (heavy) cream

salt and ground black pepper

1 Preheat the oven to 200°C/400°F/ Gas 6. Brown the guinea fowl on all sides in a roasting pan on the stove, then turn it breast uppermost and roast in the oven for 1 hour, until golden and cooked through.

2 Transfer the guinea fowl to a warmed serving dish, cover with foil and keep warm.

3 To make the sauce, pour off the excess fat from the pan, then heat the juices and stir in the whisky.

4 Bring to the boil and cook until reduced. Add the stock and cream and simmer again until reduced slightly. Strain and season to taste. Carve the guinea fowl and serve with the sauce poured over.

Nutritional information per portion: Energy 449kcal/1866kJ; Protein 34g; Carbohydrate 1g, of which sugars 1g; Fat 29g, of which saturates 13g; Cholesterol 51mg; Calcium 56mg; Fibre 0g; Sodium 200mg.

Merlot sauce for quail

Sweet, slightly tangy grapes make a tangy sauce which is excellent for accompanying quail, and here they bring a fresh fruitiness to the rich red wine sauce.

SERVES 4

4 quail, seasoned with salt and pepper
150g/5oz seedless red grapes
fresh flat leaf parsley, to garnish

FOR THE CROÛTES

4 slices white bread, crusts removed
60ml/4 tbsp olive oil

FOR THE SAUCE

50g/2oz/1/4 cup butter
4 shallots, halved
175g/6oz baby carrots, scrubbed
175g/6oz baby turnips
450ml/3/4 pint/scant 2 cups Merlot or other red wine

1 Preheat the oven to 220°C/425°F/Gas 7. Stuff the quail with grapes.

2 To make the croûtes, use a plain cutter to stamp out rounds from the bread. Heat the oil in a pan and cook the bread until golden. Drain on kitchen paper and keep warm.

3 To make the sauce, melt the butter in a heatproof casserole dish, and brown the birds. Remove the birds, set aside and keep warm.

4 Add the shallots, carrots and turnips to the fat remaining in the dish and cook until they are just beginning to colour. Replace the quail, breast sides down.

5 Pour in the wine. Cover and cook over low heat for 30 minutes, or until the quail are tender. Boil the cooking juices hard until reduced to a syrupy consistency. Skim off the fat and season. Place the quail on a croûte and serve with sauce.

Nutritional information per portion: Energy 506Kcal/2118kJ; Protein 44.6g; Carbohydrate 19.7g, of which sugars 6.8g; Fat 19.9g, of which saturates 3.7g; Cholesterol 0mg; Calcium 127mg; Fibre 2.8g; Sodium 280mg.

Port with mushroom sauce for pheasant

Marinating the pheasant in port first helps to moisten and tenderize the meat, which can often be slightly dry. If you prefer, marinate the pheasant in a full-bodied red wine.

SERVES 4

2 pheasants, cut into portions

FOR THE SAUCE

300ml/½ pint/1¼ cups port
50g/2oz/¼ cup butter
300g/11oz chestnut mushrooms, halved if large
salt and ground black pepper

1 Place the pheasant in a bowl and pour over the port. Cover and marinate for 3–4 hours or overnight.

2 Drain the meat, reserving the marinade. Pat the portions dry on kitchen paper and season.

3 Melt three-quarters of the butter in a pan and cook the pheasant portions for 5 minutes. Transfer to a plate, then cook the mushrooms in the pan for 3 minutes. Return the pheasant to the pan.

4 Pour in the reserved marinade with 200ml/7fl oz/scant 1 cup water. Bring to the boil, reduce the heat and cover, then simmer gently for about 45 minutes, until tender.

5 Remove the pheasant portions and mushrooms from the pan. Bring the cooking juices to the boil for 3–5 minutes, until reduced and thickened. Strain the juices and return to the pan. Whisk in the remaining butter then pour over the pheasant and mushrooms and serve.

Nutritional information per portion: Energy 457kcal/1902kJ; Protein 31g; Carbohydrate 9g, of which sugars 9g; Fat 24g, of which saturates 11g; Cholesterol 263mg; Calcium 46mg; Fibre 0.8g; Sodium 200mg.

Sherry and mustard sauce for pheasant

A very simple sauce to make that really adds to the flavour of the pheasant. The sauce also goes extremely well with a juicy pan-fried steak or with oven-baked chicken wrapped in ham.

SERVES 4

2 young oven-ready pheasants
50g/2oz/1/4 cup softened butter

FOR THE SAUCE

200ml/7fl oz/scant 1 cup sherry
15ml/1 tbsp Dijon mustard
salt and ground black pepper

1 Preheat the oven to 200°C/400°F/Gas 6. Put the pheasants in a roasting pan and spread the butter all over both birds. Season, then roast for 50 minutes, basting often to prevent drying out.

2 When the pheasants are cooked, take them out of the pan and leave to rest on a board, covered with foil.

3 To make the sauce, place the roasting pan over medium heat. Add the sherry and season lightly with salt and pepper.

4 Simmer for 5 minutes, until the sherry has slightly reduced, then stir in the mustard. Carve the pheasants and serve with the sherry and mustard sauce poured over.

Nutritional information per portion: Energy 393kcal/1632kJ; Protein 30g; Carbohydrate 3g, of which sugars 3g; Fat 23g, of which saturates 11g; Cholesterol 263mg; Calcium 39mg; Fibre 0g; Sodium 400mg.

Beetroot and sour cream sauce for pork

Beetroot can produce a lovely pink sauce and its rich flavour contrasts well with the sweet roasted pork. For the best results, use a piece of pork that has a small covering of fat.

SERVES 4

600g/1lb 6oz boneless pork fillet (tenderloin) or loin
1 cooked beetroot (beet), diced, to garnish

FOR THE STOCK
25ml/1½ tbsp vegetable oil
150g/5oz chicken wings
1 litre/1¾ pints/4 cups water
1 onion, chopped
1 small celery stick, chopped

FOR THE SAUCE
1 cooked beetroot (beet), diced
100ml/3½fl oz/scant ½ cup sour cream

1 To make the chicken stock, heat the oil in a large pan, add the chicken wings and fry for about 5 minutes until golden brown on all sides.

2 Add the water, onion and celery, bring to the boil, then reduce the heat and simmer for at least 1 hour. Skim off any excess fat using a slotted spoon, then strain the stock into a bowl. (This should yield about 500ml/17fl oz stock.)

3 Preheat the oven to 180°C/350°F/Gas 4. Sear the pork in a large frying pan, on its fat side, so that it starts to colour.

4 Transfer to a roasting pan and cook in the oven until tender. The time will vary depending upon the thickness of the joint but allow about 40 minutes. Put the cooked pork on a warmed serving plate and leave to rest.

5 To make the sauce, drain off any excess fat from the pan, then add the stock. Bring to the boil, stirring all the time to deglaze the pan and incorporate any sediment on the bottom of the pan.

6 Add the beetroot and the sour cream to the pan and bring to the boil. Sieve (strain) or pour the mixture into a blender or food processor and blend until the texture is smooth.

7 Pour the sauce on to individual warmed serving plates. Carefully slice the pork and place on top of the sauce, then sprinkle over the diced beetroot. Serve immediately.

Nutritional information per portion: Energy 252kcal/1056kJ; Protein 33.7g; Carbohydrate 4.8g, of which sugars 4.5g; Fat 11g, of which saturates 5.2g; Cholesterol 110mg; Calcium 44mg; Fibre 1g; Sodium 148mg.

Cider sauce for pan-fried gammon

Gammon and cider are a delicious combination, with the sweet, tangy cider complementing the gammon. The sauce can also be used as a tasty gravy for a traditional pork roast.

SERVES 4

4 gammon (smoked or cured ham) steaks, about 225g/8oz each
30ml/2 tbsp sunflower oil

FOR THE SAUCE
150ml/¼ pint/⅔ cup dry (hard) cider
45ml/3 tbsp double (heavy) cream
ground black pepper

1 Heat the oil in a large frying pan. Snip the rind and fat at intervals all around the gammon to prevent the steaks from curling up. Lay them in the pan. Cook the steaks for about 3–4 minutes on each side.

2 To make the sauce, pour the cider into the pan with the steaks. Allow to boil for a couple of minutes, then stir in the cream and cook for 1–2 minutes, until thickened. Season with pepper, and serve immediately.

Nutritional information per portion: Energy 429kcal/1784kJ; Protein 39.6g; Carbohydrate 1.2g, of which sugars 1.2g; Fat 28.4g, of which saturates 10.1g; Cholesterol 67mg; Calcium 24mg; Fibre 0g; Sodium 1985mg.

Paprika sauce for **pork**

This chunky, goulash-style dish is rich with peppers and paprika. Grilling the peppers before adding them to the sauce really brings out their sweetness.

SERVES 4

500g/1¼lb lean pork fillet (tenderloin)
2 red, 1 yellow and 1 green (bell) pepper, seeded

FOR THE SAUCE
45ml/3 tbsp paprika
300g/11oz jar or tub of tomato sauce with herbs or garlic
salt and ground black pepper

1 Preheat the grill (broiler). Cut the peppers into thick strips and sprinkle in a single layer on a foil-lined grill rack. Cook under the grill for about 20–25 minutes, until the edges of the strips are lightly charred.

2 Meanwhile, cut the pork into chunks. Season and cook in a frying pan for about 5 minutes, until beginning to brown. Then transfer the meat to a heavy pan.

3 To make the sauce, add the paprika, tomato sauce, 300ml/½ pint/1¼ cups water and a little seasoning to the pan with the meat. Bring to the boil, then reduce the heat, cover and simmer gently for 30 minutes.

4 Add the grilled (broiled) peppers and continue to cook for a further 10–15 minutes, until the meat is tender. Taste for seasoning and serve.

Nutritional information per portion: Energy 283kcal/1186kJ; Protein 33.7g; Carbohydrate 8.2g, of which sugars 8g; Fat 13g, of which saturates 1.9g; Cholesterol 42mg; Calcium 47mg; Fibre 2.3g; Sodium 304mg.

Onion and mustard sauce for pork

The piquant sauce adds plenty of punch to this simple supper dish. Serve with creamy potato mash and buttery broccoli or cabbage for the perfect feel-better meal.

SERVES 4

4 pork loin chops, 2cm/¾in thick
30ml/2 tbsp plain (all-purpose) flour
salt and ground black pepper
30ml/2 tbsp chopped fresh parsley, to garnish

FOR THE SAUCE
45ml/3 tbsp olive oil
2 Spanish (Bermuda) onions, thinly sliced
2 garlic cloves, finely chopped
250ml/8fl oz/1 cup dry (hard) cider
150ml/¼ pint/⅔ cup chicken or pork stock
generous pinch of brown sugar
2 fresh bay leaves
6 fresh thyme sprigs
2 strips lemon rind
120ml/4fl oz/½ cup double (heavy) cream
30–45ml/2–3 tbsp wholegrain mustard

1 Preheat the oven to 200°C/400°F/Gas 6. Trim the chops of excess fat. Season the flour well with salt and pepper and use to coat the chops. Heat 30ml/2 tbsp of the oil in a frying pan and brown the chops on both sides, then transfer them to an ovenproof dish.

2 To make the sauce, add the remaining oil to the pan and cook the onions over a fairly gentle heat until they soften and begin to brown. Add the chopped garlic and cook for a further 2 minutes more.

3 Stir in any left-over flour, then gradually stir in the cider and stock. Season with salt and pepper and add the brown sugar, bay leaves, thyme sprigs and lemon rind. Bring to the boil, stirring constantly, then pour over the chops.

4 Cover with foil and cook in the oven for 20 minutes. Reduce the heat to 180°C/350°F/Gas 4 and cook for a further 30–40 minutes. Remove the foil for the last 10 minutes of the cooking time.

5 Lift the chops from the sauce and transfer them to a serving dish and cover with foil. Pour the sauce from the roasting dish into a pan. Discard the herbs and lemon rind, then bring to the boil. Add the cream and continue to boil, stirring constantly. Taste for seasoning, adding a pinch more sugar if necessary. Finally, stir in the mustard to taste and pour the sauce over the braised chops. Sprinkle with the chopped parsley and serve immediately.

Nutritional information per portion: Energy 541Kcal/2235kJ; Protein 39g; Carbohydrate 19.4g, of which sugars 9g; Fat 32.9g, of which saturates 14.1g; Cholesterol 135mg; Calcium 78mg; Fibre 2g; Sodium 88mg.

Red onion relish for lamb burgers

A sharp-sweet relish of red onions, ripe little tomatoes and red peppers works well with burgers based on Middle-Eastern style lamb. Serve with pitta bread, fries and a green salad.

SERVES 4

8 lamb burgers
olive oil, for frying

FOR THE RELISH

2 red onions, cut into 5mm/¼in thick slices
75ml/5 tbsp extra virgin olive oil
2 red (bell) peppers, halved and seeded
350g/12oz cherry tomatoes, chopped
1 fresh green chilli, seeded and chopped
30ml/2 tbsp chopped fresh mint
30ml/2 tbsp chopped fresh parsley
15ml/1 tbsp chopped fresh oregano
2.5–5ml/½–1 tsp ground sumac
15ml/1 tbsp lemon juice
sugar, to taste
salt and ground black pepper

1 To make the relish, brush the onions with 15ml/1 tbsp of the oil and grill (broil) for 5 minutes each side, until brown. Cool, then chop. Grill the peppers, skinside up, until charred. Place in a bowl, cover and leave for 10 minutes. Peel, seed and finely dice the peppers and place in a large bowl.

2 Add the onions and mix. Add the tomatoes, chilli, herbs and sumac. Stir in the remaining oil and the lemon juice. Season with salt, pepper and sugar.

3 Heat a heavy frying pan or a ridged, cast-iron griddle pan over high heat and grease lightly with olive oil. Cook the burgers for about 5–6 minutes on each side, or until just cooked at the centre.

4 While the burgers are cooking, taste the relish and adjust the seasoning. Serve the burgers freshly cooked, with the relish.

Nutritional information per portion: Energy 514kcal/2135kJ; Protein 27.4g; Carbohydrate 19.1g, of which sugars 13.5g; Fat 37g, of which saturates 10.7g; Cholesterol 96mg; Calcium 96mg; Fibre 4.5g; Sodium 107mg.

Quick mustard sauce for **lamb chops**

This is a popular way to serve lamb in England. To make a richer and creamier tasting sauce, add 150ml/¼ pint/⅔ cup sour cream when you add the mustard in step 3.

SERVES 4

15ml/1 tbsp tender rosemary leaves
60ml/4 tbsp olive oil
4 Barnsley chops or 8 lamb loin chops
salt and ground black pepper

FOR THE SAUCE

100ml/3½fl oz/scant ½ cup lamb or beef stock
30ml/2 tbsp wholegrain mustard
5ml/1 tsp Worcestershire sauce

1 Chop the rosemary very finely and mix with the oil. Rub the mixture over the chops and leave to stand, covered, for 30 minutes, or longer if refrigerated. Season lightly with salt and pepper.

2 Heat a large frying pan, add the chops and cook over medium heat for 5–8 minutes on each side then lift the chops out of the pan, and keep warm.

3 To make the sauce, pour the stock into the hot pan, scraping up any sediment, and add the mustard. Heat until the mixture comes to the boil and leave to bubble gently until reduced by about one third.

4 Stir in the Worcestershire sauce and adjust the seasoning. Serve the chops with the mustard sauce spooned over.

Nutritional information per portion: Energy 582kcal/2401kJ; Protein 18.8g; Carbohydrate 0.9g, of which sugars 0.8g; Fat 55.9g, of which saturates 23.6g; Cholesterol 96mg; Calcium 17mg; Fibre 0g; Sodium 313mg.

Creamy dill sauce for lamb

Lamb and boiled new potatoes are partnered with this classic Swedish dill sauce, but it is also delicious with salmon or prawns. The sauce can also be used to liven up leafy salads.

SERVES 6–8

1kg/2¼lb lamb neck fillet or boned leg, cubed
1 Spanish (Bermuda) onion, roughly chopped
1 carrot, chopped
1 celery stick, chopped
1 bay leaf
2 sprigs fresh thyme
boiled new potatoes, to serve

FOR THE SAUCE
1 bunch fresh dill
250ml/8fl oz/1 cup water
90g/3½oz/½ cup sugar
120ml/4fl oz/½ cup white vinegar
10g/¼oz/½ tbsp butter, softened
10g/¼oz/½ tbsp plain (all-purpose) flour
1 egg yolk
120ml/4fl oz/½ cup double (heavy) cream
salt and ground black pepper

1 Put the cubed lamb in a large pan and then add the onion, carrot, celery, bay leaf and thyme. Pour in enough cold water to cover the ingredients fully, bring to simmering point and then simmer for about 40 minutes to 1 hour until the meat is tender.

2 To make the sauce, remove the dill fronds from the main stalks, reserving the stalks, chop finely and set aside. Put the reserved stalks in a pan and add the water, sugar and vinegar. Bring to the boil then boil for 5 minutes.

3 Meanwhile, put the butter in a bowl and work in the flour with a fork until smooth to make a beurre manié. Mix the egg yolk and cream together.

4 When the lamb is cooked, put 1 litre/1¾ pints/4 cups of the stock from the lamb in a pan. Strain in the sugar and vinegar liquid then bring the mixture to simmering point. Add small knobs (pats) of the beurre manié, whisking vigorously, and allow each knob to melt before adding another, to thicken the sauce. Bring to the boil then simmer for about 10 minutes.

5 Stir the egg and cream mixture and the chopped dill fronds into the sauce. Do not allow the mixture to boil or the sauce will curdle. Pour the sauce over the lamb, and serve with the potatoes.

Nutritional information per portion: Energy 509kcal/2125kJ; Protein 34.4g; Carbohydrate 22.6g, of which sugars 20.1g; Fat 31.8g, of which saturates 16g; Cholesterol 191mg; Calcium 56mg; Fibre 1.2g; Sodium 169mg.

Creamy redcurrant sauce for meatloaf

Gravy is subtly sweetened with redcurrant jelly, and served alongside buttery fans of Hasselback potatoes and meatloaf to make a rich and luxurious meal.

SERVES 6

450g/1lb lean minced (ground) beef
450g/1lb minced (ground) pork
75g/3oz/1½ cups fine breadcrumbs
25g/1oz/2 tbsp finely chopped onion
2 eggs
75ml/5 tbsp double (heavy) cream
3–4 streaky (fatty) bacon rashers (strips)
salt and ground black pepper

FOR THE HASSELBACK POTATOES

12 medium-sized oval or round potatoes (about 1.8kg/4 lb total weight)
50g/2oz/¼ cup butter
25g/1oz/½ cup fine breadcrumbs
25g/1oz/⅓ cup freshly grated Parmesan cheese
salt and white pepper

FOR THE SAUCE

15g/½oz/1 tbsp butter
25g/1oz/¼ cup plain (all-purpose) flour
120ml/4fl oz/½ cup single (light) cream
60ml/4 tbsp redcurrant jelly

1 Preheat the oven to 190°C/375°F/Gas 5. Put the minced beef and pork in a large bowl and mix together thoroughly. Stir in the breadcrumbs, chopped onion, eggs, cream, salt and pepper.

2 Turn the mixture into a 12.5 x 23cm/5 x 9in loaf tin (pan), pressing it in firmly, and arrange the bacon rashers over the top. Bake for 1 hour.

3 Meanwhile, lightly grease a baking dish. Peel the potatoes and rinse under cold water. Cut each potato crossways into 12–15 thin, even slices, taking care not to cut all the way through to the bottom, so the slices hold together.

4 Place the potatoes, sliced side up, in the prepared baking dish. Dot evenly with butter, and sprinkle with salt and pepper.

5 Roast for about 1–1½ hours, or until tender and light brown, basting with butter during cooking. Sprinkle with breadcrumbs and grated cheese 20 minutes before the end of the cooking time.

6 When the meatloaf is cooked through, pour off the fat and reserve. Leave the loaf to cool for about 15 minutes while you make the sauce.

7 To make the sauce, pour 75ml/2½fl oz/⅓ cup of reserved fat into a pan. Add the butter and heat until it melts. Whisk in the flour, and cook, stirring, for 2–4 minutes until well blended. Stir in the cream, redcurrant jelly, salt and pepper. Cook until smooth and heated through.

8 Carefully slice the meatloaf and place on warmed serving plates. Serve drizzled with the creamy redcurrant sauce over, and accompanied by the Hasselback potatoes.

Nutritional information per portion: Energy 935kcal/3903kJ; Protein 41.2g; Carbohydrate 69.2g, of which sugars 12.1g; Fat 56.7g, of which saturates 28.6g; Cholesterol 199mg; Calcium 136mg; Fibre 3.5g; Sodium 478mg.

Brandy sauce for **steak**

Fried steak, sizzling in its own juices and served with a delicious brandy-flavoured sauce that doubles as a marinade, makes a luxurious supper to remember.

SERVES 2

2 rump (round) or sirloin steaks, total weight about 450g/1lb
15–30ml/1–2 tbsp vegetable oil
shredded spring onion (scallion), to garnish

FOR THE SAUCE

15ml/1 tbsp brandy
15ml/1 tbsp rich brown sauce
30ml/2 tbsp groundnut (peanut) oil or sunflower oil
a few drops of sesame oil
2 garlic cloves, halved or crushed
150ml/1/4 pint/2/3 cup beef stock
30ml/2 tbsp tomato ketchup
15ml/1 tbsp oyster sauce
15ml/1 tbsp Worcestershire sauce
salt and sugar

1 Put the steaks side by side in a bowl. Mix the brandy, brown sauce, groundnut or sunflower oil, sesame oil and garlic in a jug (pitcher) and pour this marinade over the steaks.

2 Cover loosely with clear film (plastic wrap) and leave for 1 hour. Drain well, reserving the marinade.

3 Heat the oil in a heavy, ridged griddle pan and cook the steaks for 3–5 minutes on each side, depending on how well done you like them. Transfer to a plate.

4 Pour the marinade into the griddle pan, discarding any large pieces of garlic, if you like.

5 Stir in the beef stock, ketchup, oyster sauce and Worcestershire sauce, with salt and sugar to taste. Bring to the boil, and boil rapidly to reduce by half, then taste again for seasoning.

6 Serve each cooked steak on a hot plate, pouring the sauce over each portion just before serving. Garnish with the shredded spring onion.

Nutritional information per portion: Energy 469kcal/1956kJ; Protein 53.1g; Carbohydrate 4.1g, of which sugars 3.8g; Fat 26.7g, of which saturates 7.4g; Cholesterol 115mg; Calcium 20mg; Fibre 0.1g; Sodium 409mg.

Warm tomato salsa for steak

A easy-to-make, refreshing, tangy salsa of tomatoes, spring onions and balsamic vinegar makes a tasty and colourful topping for chunky, pan-fried steaks.

SERVES 2

2 steaks, about 2cm/¾ in thick
salt and ground black pepper

FOR THE SALSA

4 large plum tomatoes
2 spring onions (scallions)
30ml/2 tbsp balsamic vinegar
30ml/2 tbsp water

1 Trim any excess fat from the steaks, then season on both sides with salt and pepper. Heat a non-stick frying pan and cook the steaks for about 3 minutes on each side for medium rare. Cook for a little longer if you like your steak well cooked.

2 For the salsa, put the tomatoes in a heatproof bowl, cover with boiling water and leave for 1–2 minutes, until the skins start to split.

3 Drain and peel the tomatoes, then halve them and scoop out the seeds. Dice the tomato flesh. Then thinly slice the spring onions.

4 Transfer the steaks to plates and keep warm. Add the balsamic vinegar, water and a little seasoning to the cooking juices in the pan and stir briefly until warm, scraping up any meat residue. Serve the salsa over the steaks.

Nutritional information per portion: Energy 175kcal/736kJ; Protein 25g; Carbohydrate 3g, of which sugars 7g; Fat 3g, of which saturates 69g; Cholesterol 69mg; Calcium 18mg; Fibre 0.9g; Sodium 100mg.

Creamy white sauce for smoked beef

This unusual recipe draws on the Irish heritage of potato pancakes and fine smoked meats. Chargrilled beef fillet is a delicious alternative to the turf-smoked original.

SERVES 4

500g/1$^{1}/_{4}$lb trimmed beef fillet
oil, for chargrilling
salt and ground black pepper
herb sprigs, to garnish
broccoli florets, white turnip and courgettes (zucchini), to serve

FOR THE POTATO PANCAKES
250g/9oz potatoes, cooked
50g/2oz/$^{1}/_{2}$ cup plain (all-purpose) flour
1 egg
freshly grated nutmeg
oil, for frying

FOR THE SAUCE
4 shallots, finely diced
200ml/7fl oz/scant 1 cup chicken stock
120ml/4fl oz/$^{1}/_{2}$ cup white wine
200ml/7fl oz/scant 1 cup double (heavy) cream
15ml/1 tbsp chopped fresh herbs, such as flat leaf parsley, tarragon, chervil and basil
lemon juice, to taste

1 To make the potato pancakes, blend the potatoes with the flour and egg to make a thick purée. Add nutmeg and seasoning to taste.

2 Lightly oil and heat a heavy pan, then use the potato purée to make eight small pancakes, cooking them on both sides until golden brown. Keep warm.

3 To make the sauce, put the shallots, stock, wine and half the cream into a pan and cook over medium heat until they are reduced by two-thirds. Purée the mixture and strain it, then mix in enough herbs to turn the sauce green.

4 Season the beef with salt and freshly ground black pepper. In a heavy, preheated pan, seal the meat on all sides over medium heat.

5 Place the meat in a smoker for about 10 minutes until medium-rare. Or, to chargrill the meat, preheat a ridged pan until hot. Brush the meat with oil and cook for 3–5 minutes, turning once.

6 To serve, whip the remaining cream and fold it into the sauce, adjusting the seasoning and adding lemon juice if required. Divide the sauce between four warm plates. Cut the beef into eight slices and place two slices on each plate. Arrange the pancakes around the meat. Garnish with herbs and serve with the broccoli, turnip and courgettes, if using.

Nutritional information per portion: Energy 683kcal/2834kJ; Protein 32.9g; Carbohydrate 23g, of which sugars 3g; Fat 49.5g, of which saturates 27.5g; Cholesterol 219mg; Calcium 82mg; Fibre 1.9g; Sodium 166mg.

Stout sauce for **pot-roast beef**

This method is ideal for cuts that need tenderizing by long, slow cooking in a rich sauce. Boned and rolled joints such as brisket, silverside and topside of beef are perfect.

SERVES 6

30ml/2 tbsp vegetable oil
900g/2lb rolled brisket of beef
2 medium onions, roughly chopped
2 celery sticks, thickly sliced
450g/1lb carrots, cut into large chunks
675g/1½lb potatoes, peeled and cut into large chunks

FOR THE SAUCE

30ml/2 tbsp plain (all-purpose) flour
450ml/¾ pint/scant 2 cups beef stock
300ml/½ pint/1¼ cups stout
1 bay leaf
45ml/3 tbsp chopped fresh thyme
5ml/1 tsp soft light brown sugar
30ml/2 tbsp wholegrain mustard
15ml/1 tbsp tomato purée (paste)
salt and ground black pepper

1 Preheat the oven to 180°C/350°F/Gas 4. Heat the oil in a large flameproof casserole dish and brown the beef until golden brown all over. Lift the beef from the pan and drain on kitchen paper.

2 Add the onions to the pan and cook for about 4 minutes, until just beginning to soften and brown. Add the celery, carrots and potatoes to the dish and cook over medium heat for 2–3 minutes, until they are just beginning to colour.

3 To make the sauce, add the flour to the dish and cook for a minute, stirring continuously. Gradually pour in the beef stock and the stout. Heat until boiling, stirring frequently. Stir in the bay leaf, thyme, sugar, mustard, tomato purée and season.

4 Place the meat on top, cover and transfer to the oven. Cook for 2½ hours, or until tender. Season to taste. To serve, slice the beef and pour the sauce on top.

Nutritional information per portion: Energy 415kcal/1743kJ; Protein 36g; Carbohydrate 35.6g, of which sugars 13.1g; Fat 14g, of which saturates 4.4g; Cholesterol 81mg; Calcium 66mg; Fibre 4.2g; Sodium 284mg.

Sour cherry sauce for venison

Served mainly in autumn or winter during the hunting season, venison's rich flavour and earthy taste marry extremely well with the sweetness of the cherries.

SERVES 4–6

2–2.5kg/4½–5½lb venison tenderloin
25g/1oz/2 tbsp butter, softened
250ml/8fl oz/1 cup water
salt and ground black pepper

FOR THE SAUCE
250ml/8fl oz/1 cup cherry juice
120ml/4fl oz/½ cup water
25ml/1½ tbsp cornflour (cornstarch)
425g/15oz canned or frozen unsweetened stoned (pitted) cherries
90g/3½oz/½ cup sugar, or to taste

1 Preheat the oven to 230°C/450°F/Gas 8. Tie the venison at 2.5cm/1in intervals with fine string to hold its shape while roasting.

2 Sprinkle with salt and pepper, and spread with butter. Place on a rack in a roasting pan, and add the water. Cook for 20 minutes to brown.

3 Lower the heat to 180°C/350°F/Gas 4. Cook, basting at intervals with the pan juices, for 1¼ hours, until barely pink in the centre.

4 Leave the browned meat to rest for 10 minutes before slicing.

5 To make the sauce, bring the cherry juice to the boil in a pan over medium-high heat. Whisk together the water and cornflour in a small bowl, and stir into the cherry juice.

6 Cook the sauce, stirring constantly, until the mixture thickens. Stir in the cherries and bring the mixture back to the boil. Serve with the venison.

Nutritional information per portion: Energy 518kcal/2197kJ; Protein 74.6g; Carbohydrate 37.5g, of which sugars 33.7g; Fat 10.8g, of which saturates 4.8g; Cholesterol 176mg; Calcium 45mg; Fibre 0.4g; Sodium 220mg.

Juniper berry sauce for braised hare

This fruity sauce gives this hare stew a wonderful taste without overpowering the meat. If you cannot find juniper berries, substitute them with cranberries.

SERVES 6–8

25g/1oz/2 tbsp butter
15ml/1 tbsp vegetable oil
1 oven-ready hare (jackrabbit), cut into pieces
parsley sprigs, to garnish
rowanberry jelly and pickled cucumbers, to serve (optional)

FOR THE SAUCE

1 onion, roughly chopped
1 carrot, roughly chopped
2 celery sticks, roughly chopped
200ml/7fl oz/scant 1 cup red wine
15ml/1 tbsp blackcurrant jelly
8 juniper berries, crushed
1 fresh thyme sprig and 1 bay leaf
475ml/16fl oz/2 cups water
15ml/1 tbsp plain (all-purpose) flour
200ml/7fl oz/scant 1 cup double (heavy) cream
salt and ground black pepper

1 Melt 15g/½oz/1 tbsp of the butter with the vegetable oil in a large, heavy pan. Add the hare joints and fry for about 15 minutes until browned.

2 Add the onion, carrot, celery, red wine, blackcurrant jelly, juniper berries, thyme, bay leaf, salt and pepper to the pan with the hare joints. Bring to the boil then simmer until the wine has almost evaporated.

3 Add the water, cover and simmer for a further 35 minutes until the meat is tender, adding more water if necessary to prevent it from becoming dry. Transfer the meat to a warmed serving dish, cover with foil and keep warm.

4 Strain the stock through a sieve (strainer) into a clean pan. Put the remaining butter in a small bowl and beat until soft. Add the flour and blend together to form a smooth paste.

5 Heat the stock in the pan and add small pieces of the butter mixture, whisking or stirring vigorously until each piece has melted before adding another piece. Bring to the boil then simmer, stirring all the time, until the sauce becomes creamy. Then stir in the double cream.

6 Divide the meat on to warmed serving plates and pour the sauce over. Garnish with parsley sprigs and serve with rowanberry jelly and pickled cucumbers, if using.

Nutritional information per portion: Energy 336kcal/1400kJ; Protein 25.5g; Carbohydrate 4.7g, of which sugars 3g; Fat 22.3g, of which saturates 12.4g; Cholesterol 101mg; Calcium 50mg; Fibre 0.5g; Sodium 109mg.

Roasted peanut and quince sauce for rabbit

Rabbit meat can be deep-fried, roasted, or enjoyed in stews like this one. The buttery, earthy taste of the roasted peanuts combines perfectly with the freshness of the quince.

SERVES 4

4 rabbit leg joints
250ml/8fl oz/1 cup red wine vinegar
2 rosemary sprigs
10ml/2 tsp ground paprika
4 garlic cloves, crushed
2.5ml/½ tsp ground black pepper
60ml/4 tbsp vegetable oil
salt

FOR THE SAUCE

250ml/8fl oz/1 cup white wine
250ml/8fl oz/1 cup water
1 quince or large cooking apple, peeled and sliced
200g/7oz/1¾ cups roasted, salted peanuts, ground in a blender

1 Put the rabbit joints in a bowl with the vinegar, rosemary, paprika, garlic, black pepper and salt and leave to marinate for 2 hours.

2 Heat the vegetable oil in a frying pan over high heat. Dry the pieces of rabbit and fry on each side, until browned all over.

3 Add the white wine and the water to the pan. Then add the slices of quince or cooking apple and the peanuts. Bring to the boil then reduce the heat to medium, cover the pan and simmer for 30 minutes, until the rabbit is tender.

4 Serve the rabbit in individual warmed serving bowls with rice or boiled potatoes and lots of sauce spooned on top.

Nutritional information per portion: Energy 559kcal/2324kJ; Protein 35.2g; Carbohydrate 9g, of which sugars 5g; Fat 38.3g, of which saturates 6.9g; Cholesterol 71mg; Calcium 63mg; Fibre 3.4g; Sodium 72mg.

White caper sauce for veal meatballs

The mild, creamy sauce complements the veal very well in this classic German dish. The capers give it a special character but if you don't like them, they can be omitted.

SERVES 4

2 day-old white bread rolls, about 100g/3¾oz total weight
1kg/2¼lb minced (ground) veal
2 onions, finely chopped
2 anchovies, finely chopped
10ml/2 tsp capers, chopped
15ml/1 tbsp chopped parsley
5ml/1 tsp medium-hot mustard
2 eggs
salt and ground white pepper
boiled rice, to serve

FOR THE SAUCE

200ml/7fl oz/scant 1 cup single (light) cream
50g/2oz/¼ cup butter
50g/2oz/½ cup plain (all-purpose) flour
10ml/2 tsp capers

1 Soak the bread rolls in water, then squeeze them out, break into small pieces and place in a mixing bowl. Add the veal, onions and anchovies. Add the capers to the bowl, with 5ml/1 tsp of the parsley and the mustard. Season, then add the eggs and mix well. Form into 12–14 meatballs.

2 Bring a pan of salted water to the boil over high heat and add the meatballs. Reduce the heat and leave to simmer for 8–10 minutes. Remove the meatballs, reserving the stock, and keep them warm in a low oven.

3 Transfer 500ml/17fl oz/generous 2 cups of the stock to a pan and bring it to the boil. Stir in the cream. Knead the butter with the flour to make a beurre manié and stir into the mixture, a little at a time, until it is thickened.

4 Add the capers and let the sauce cook for 3 minutes, then add the meatballs back. Garnish with the remaining parsley and serve with rice.

Nutritional information per portion: Energy 722kcal/3018kJ; Protein 59.9g; Carbohydrate 30.1g, of which sugars 7.2g; Fat 41.2g, of which saturates 20.9g; Cholesterol 306mg; Calcium 160mg; Fibre 2g; Sodium 554mg.

Wheat beer sauce for veal

Wheat beers are made in Bavaria, Belgium and northern France, where they are known as bières blanches or white beers. The slight bitterness that the beer gives the sauce in this delectable stew is matched by the sweetness of the caramelized onions and carrots.

SERVES 4

45ml/3 tbsp plain (all-purpose) flour
900g/2lb boned shoulder or leg of veal, cut into 5cm/2in cubes
60g/2½oz/5 tbsp butter
3 shallots, finely chopped
salt and ground black pepper

FOR THE SAUCE

1 celery stick
fresh parsley sprig
2 fresh bay leaves
5ml/1 tsp caster (superfine) sugar, plus a good pinch
200ml/7fl oz/scant 1 cup wheat beer
450ml/¾ pint/scant 2 cups veal stock
20–25 large silverskin onions or pickling (pearl) onions
450g/1lb carrots, thickly sliced
2 large egg yolks
105ml/7 tbsp double (heavy) cream
30ml/2 tbsp chopped fresh parsley

1 Season the flour and dust the veal in it. Heat 25g/1oz/2 tbsp of the butter in a deep, lidded frying pan, add the veal and quickly seal it on all sides. The veal should be golden but not dark brown. Use a draining spoon to remove the veal from the pan and set aside.

2 Reduce the heat, add another 15g/½oz/1 tbsp butter to the pan and cook the shallots gently for 5–6 minutes, until soft and yellow. Replace the veal.

3 To make the sauce, tie the celery, parsley and 1 bay leaf together in a bundle, then add them to the pan with a good pinch of caster sugar.

4 Increase the heat, pour in the beer and allow to bubble briefly before pouring in the stock. Season, bring to the boil, then cover and simmer gently, stirring once or twice, for 40–50 minutes, or until the veal is cooked.

5 Meanwhile, melt the remaining butter in another frying pan and add the onions, then fry them over low heat until golden all over. Remove the onions from the pan and set aside.

6 Add the carrots and turn to coat them in the butter remaining from the onions. Stir in 5ml/1 tsp caster sugar, a pinch of salt, the remaining bay leaf and enough water to cover the carrots. Bring to the boil and simmer uncovered for 10–12 minutes until part cooked.

7 Return the onions to the pan with the carrots and continue to cook until all but a few tablespoons of the liquid has evaporated and the onions and carrots are slightly caramelized. Keep warm. Transfer the veal to a bowl and discard the celery and herb bundle.

8 Beat the egg yolks and cream together in another bowl, then beat in a ladleful of the hot, but not boiling, carrot liquid. Return this mixture to the pan and cook over very low heat without boiling, stirring until thickened a little.

9 Add the veal, onions and carrots to the sauce. Reheat and adjust the seasoning, then serve with the sauce spooned over the top, and sprinkle with the parsley.

Nutritional information per portion: Energy 660kcal/2752kJ; Protein 52.8g; Carbohydrate 27.8g, of which sugars 16.6g; Fat 37.1g, of which saturates 20.2g; Cholesterol 360mg; Calcium 140mg; Fibre 4.9g; Sodium 399mg.

Sauces for sweet dishes

Dessert sauces are the ultimate sweet treat. Fruit sauces bursting with flavour are divine served on dairy desserts; lusciously dark chocolate sauces bring bitter-sweet intrigue to ice creams, while zesty citrus infusions transform crisp waffles and pancakes into an exotic sweet course. There are also custards, syrups and caramels, so there is something for everyone.

Real custard

Adding cornflour helps to prevent custard from curdling. This recipe uses enough cornflour to ensure success, and makes a sumptuous custard that is good with all kinds of hot puddings.

SERVES 4–6

450ml/¾ pint/scant 2 cups milk
few drops of vanilla extract
2 eggs plus 1 egg yolk
15–30ml/1–2 tbsp caster (superfine) sugar
15ml/1 tbsp cornflour (cornstarch)
30ml/2 tbsp water

1 In a small pan heat the milk with the vanilla extract and remove from the heat just as the milk comes to the boil.

2 Whisk the eggs and yolk in a bowl with the sugar until combined but not frothy. In a separate bowl, blend together the cornflour with the water and mix into the eggs. Whisk in a little of the milk, then mix in all the remaining milk.

3 Strain the egg and milk mixture back into the pan and gently heat, stirring the mixture constantly with a wooden spoon. Take care not to overheat the mixture or the eggs will curdle.

4 Continue stirring until the custard thickens sufficiently to coat the back of a wooden spoon. Do not allow to boil or it will curdle. Serve the hot custard immediately.

Nutritional information per portion: Energy 156Kcal/656kJ; Protein 8g; Carbohydrate 17.9g, of which sugars 11g; Fat 6.5g, of which saturates 2.4g; Cholesterol 170mg; Calcium 147mg; Fibre 0g; Sodium 92mg.

Dulce de leche

Spanish in origin, this toffee-like dessert is a children's favourite throughout Latin America. It is traditionally made with milk and sugar, but this version is much quicker and just as delicious.

SERVES 6

400g/14oz can sweetened condensed milk
400g/14oz can evaporated milk

1 Combine the condensed and evaporated milk together in a large heavy pan. Place over medium heat and bring the mixture to the boil, then reduce the heat.

2 Cook for 30–35 minutes, stirring constantly, until thickened and toffee coloured.

3 Pour into a sterilized jar and seal. Dulce de leche will keep for months, but with time, the texture will alter and won't be as smooth.

4 Serve the sauce with ice cream, as a filling for warmed pancakes or cakes, or even with a white cheese, such as ricotta.

Nutritional information per portion: Energy 323kcal/1357kJ; Protein 11.3g; Carbohydrate 42.7g, of which sugars 42.7g; Fat 13g, of which saturates 8.1g; Cholesterol 47mg; Calcium 387mg; Fibre 0g; Sodium 210mg.

Vanilla cream for apple cake

Apples are very sweet and ideally suited to this sublime cake, and the light, creamy sauce is the perfect accompaniment. For a tangy version substitute strips of orange rind for the vanilla pod.

SERVES 6–8

115g/4 oz/1/2 cup plus 15ml/1 tbsp unsalted (sweet) butter
7 eating apples
30ml/2 tbsp caster (superfine) sugar
10ml/2 tsp ground cinnamon
200g/7oz/1 cup sugar
2 egg yolks and 3 egg whites
100g/3 3/4oz/1 cup ground almonds
grated rind and juice of 1/2 lemon

FOR THE SAUCE
250ml/8fl oz/1 cup milk
250ml/8fl oz/1 cup double (heavy) cream
15ml/1 tbsp sugar
1 vanilla pod (bean), split
4 egg yolks, beaten

1 Preheat the oven to 180°C/350°F/Gas 4. Butter a 20cm/8in flan tin (pan) using 15g/1/2oz/1 tbsp of the butter. Peel, core and thinly slice the apples and put the slices in a bowl. Add the caster sugar and cinnamon and mix them together. Put the mixture in the prepared tin.

2 Put the remaining butter and sugar in a bowl and whisk them together until they are light and fluffy. Beat in the egg yolks, then add the almonds and lemon rind and juice to the mixture.

3 Whisk the egg whites until stiff then fold into the mixture. Pour the mixture over the apples in the flan tin. Bake in the oven for about 40 minutes until golden brown and the apples are tender.

4 Meanwhile, make the vanilla cream. Put the milk, cream, sugar and vanilla pod in a pan and heat gently. Add a little of the warm milk mixture to the egg yolks then slowly add the egg mixture to the pan and continue to heat gently, stirring all the time, until the mixture thickens. Do not allow the mixture to boil or it will curdle.

5 Remove the vanilla pod and serve the vanilla cream warm or cold with the apple cake.

Nutritional information per portion: Energy 541kcal/2254kJ; Protein 7.6g; Carbohydrate 39.7g, of which sugars 39.3g; Fat 40.3g, of which saturates 20g; Cholesterol 227mg; Calcium 122mg; Fibre 2.1g; Sodium 135mg.

Simple chocolate sauce for poached pears

Many types of pear are available, and for a refreshing treat they can be simply eaten raw or gently poached and served with a rich chocolate sauce, as in this recipe.

SERVES 4

4 firm dessert pears, peeled
250g/9oz/1¼ cups caster (superfine) sugar
600ml/1 pint/2½ cups water
500ml/17fl oz/generous 2 cups vanilla ice cream

FOR THE SAUCE

250g/9oz good quality dark (bittersweet) chocolate (minimum 70 per cent cocoa solids)
40g/1½oz unsalted (sweet) butter
5ml/1 tsp vanilla extract
75ml/5 tbsp double (heavy) cream

1 Cut the pears in half lengthways and remove the core. Place the sugar and water in a large pan and gently heat until the sugar has dissolved completely.

2 Add the pear halves to the pan, then simmer for about 20 minutes, or until the pears are tender but not falling apart. Lift out of the sugar syrup with a slotted spoon and leave to cool.

3 To make the chocolate sauce, break the chocolate into small pieces and put into a pan. Add the butter and 30ml/2 tbsp water. Heat gently over low heat, without stirring, until the chocolate has melted. Add the vanilla extract and cream, and mix gently.

4 Place a scoop of ice cream into each serving bowl. Add two cooled pear halves and pour over the sauce.

Nutritional information per portion: Energy 1014kcal/4255kJ; Protein 8.8g; Carbohydrate 145.1g, of which sugars 143.2g; Fat 46.7g, of which saturates 29.6g; Cholesterol 81mg; Calcium 206mg; Fibre 4.9g; Sodium 152mg.

Marsala sauce for baked apples

The Marsala cooks down with the juice from the apples and the butter to make a rich, sticky sauce. Serve these delicious apples with a spoonful of extra-thick cream.

SERVES 4

4 medium cooking apples
50g/2oz/1/3 cup ready-to-eat dried figs

FOR THE SAUCE

50g/2oz/1/4 cup butter, softened
150ml/1/4 pint/2/3 cup Marsala

1 Preheat the oven to 180°C/350°F/Gas 4. Using an apple corer, remove the apple cores and discard.

2 Place the apples in a shallow roasting pan and stuff the figs into the holes in each apple.

3 To make the sauce, top each apple with a quarter of the butter and pour over the Marsala.

4 Cover the roasting pan with foil and bake for about 30 minutes.

5 Remove the foil from the apples and bake for a further 10 minutes, or until the apples are tender and the sauce has reduced slightly.

6 Serve immediately while hot with the remaining sauce drizzled over the top.

Nutritional information per portion: Energy 722kcal/3003kJ; Protein 62.1g; Carbohydrate 2.9g, of which sugars 2.5g; Fat 48.8g, of which saturates 26.6g; Cholesterol 278mg; Calcium 66mg; Fibre 0.7g; Sodium 171mg.

Mixed berry sauce for ricotta cakes

This fabulously fragrant, fruity sauce complements ice creams, custards, sponge puddings and cheesecakes – especially these honey and vanilla baked ricotta cheesecakes.

SERVES 4

250g/9oz/generous 1 cup ricotta cheese
2 egg whites
about 60ml/4 tbsp clear honey
few drops of vanilla extract
fresh mint leaves, to decorate (optional)

FOR THE SAUCE

450g/1lb/4 cups mixed fresh or frozen fruit, such as strawberries, raspberries, blackberries and cherries

1 Preheat the oven to 180°C/350°F/Gas 4. Grease four ramekins.

2 Place the ricotta cheese in a bowl and break it up with a wooden spoon. Lightly whisk the egg whites with a fork to break them up, then mix into the cheese with the honey and vanilla until combined and smooth.

3 Spoon the ricotta mixture into the prepared ramekins and level the tops. Bake for 20 minutes or until golden.

4 To make the berry sauce. Reserve about a quarter of the fruit for decoration. Place the rest of the fruit in a pan, with a little water if the fruit is fresh, and heat gently until softened. Cool slightly, removing any cherry stones (pits).

5 Strain the fruit through, then taste and sweeten with honey if it is tart. Serve the sauce, warm or cold, with the ricotta cakes. Decorate with the reserved berries and mint.

Nutritional information per portion: Energy 186kcal/782kJ; Protein 8.7g; Carbohydrate 18g, of which sugars 18g; Fat 9.4g, of which saturates 5.8g; Cholesterol 26mg; Calcium 27mg; Fibre 2.5g; Sodium 35mg.

Papaya sauce for grilled pineapple

This sweet papaya sauce partners slightly tart fruit perfectly – pineapple, redcurrants or gooseberries. It is also excellent when served with grilled chicken, game birds, pork or lamb.

SERVES 6

1 sweet pineapple, peeled, cored, cut into 2.5cm/1in thick slices
melted butter, for greasing and brushing
2 pieces drained preserved stem ginger in syrup, cut into fine matchstick pieces
30ml/2 tbsp demerara (raw) sugar
pinch of ground cinnamon
30ml/2 tbsp preserved stem ginger syrup
fresh mint sprigs, to decorate

FOR THE SAUCE

1 ripe papaya, peeled and seeded
175ml/6fl oz/3/4 cup apple juice

1 Line a baking tray with a sheet of foil, rolling up the edges to make a rim. Grease the foil with melted butter. Preheat the grill (broiler).

2 To make the sauce, cut a few slices from the papaya and set them aside. Then purée the rest with the apple juice in a food processor.

3 Press the purée through a fine sieve (strainer) and set aside.

4 Arrange the pineapple slices on the foil. Brush with butter, then top with the ginger and sprinkle with the sugar and cinnamon. Drizzle over the ginger syrup. Grill (broil) for 5–7 minutes, or until the slices are lightly charred.

5 Arrange the pineapple slices on warm plates and drizzle over the sauce. Decorate with the reserved papaya slices and the mint sprigs.

Nutritional information per portion: Energy 110kcal/469kJ; Protein 0.9g; Carbohydrate 27.5g, of which sugars 27.5g; Fat 0.4g, of which saturates 0g; Cholesterol 0mg; Calcium 44mg; Fibre 3.1g; Sodium 7mg.

Amaretto sauce for peaches

The apricot and almond flavour of the amaretto liqueur subtly enhances the sweet, fruity taste of ripe peaches. Serve with a spoonful of crème fraîche or whipped cream.

SERVES 4

4 ripe peaches
crème fraîche or whipped cream, to serve

FOR THE SAUCE
45ml/3 tbsp Amaretto di Sarone liqueur
45ml/3 tbsp clear honey

1 Preheat the oven to 190°C/ 375°F/Gas 5. Cut the peaches in half and prise out the stones (pits) with a knife. Place the peaches cut side up in a pan.

2 To make the sauce, place the amaretto liqueur and the honey in a small bowl and mix together.

3 Drizzle the sauce over the peaches, covering them evenly, then bake the peaches in the oven for 20–25 minutes, or until tender.

4 To serve, place two peach halves on each serving plate and drizzle with the pan juices. Serve immediately while hot.

Nutritional information per portion: Energy 111kcal/472kJ; Protein 2g; Carbohydrate 24g, of which sugars 6g; Fat 1g, of which saturates 1g; Cholesterol 4mg; Calcium 72mg; Fibre 0.4g; Sodium 100mg.

Toffee sauce for baked bananas and ice cream

Bananas make one of the easiest of all desserts, just as welcome as a comforting winter treat. For an extra sweet sauce, grate some plain chocolate into the sauce just before serving.

SERVES 4

4 large bananas
4 scoops good-quality vanilla ice cream

FOR THE SAUCE

75g/3oz/scant 1/2 cup light muscovado (brown) sugar
75ml/5 tbsp double (heavy) cream

1 Preheat the oven to 180°C/ 350°F/Gas 4. Put the unpeeled bananas in an ovenproof dish and bake for 15–20 minutes, until the skins are very dark and the flesh feels soft when squeezed.

2 To make the sauce, heat the light muscovado sugar in a small, heavy pan with 75ml/5 tbsp water until dissolved.

3 Bring to the boil and add the double cream. Cook for 5 minutes, until the sauce has thickened and is toffee coloured. Remove from the heat.

4 Transfer the baked bananas in their skins to serving plates and split them lengthways to reveal the flesh. Pour some of the sauce over the bananas and top with scoops of vanilla ice cream. Serve any remaining sauce separately.

Nutritional information per portion: Energy 368kcal/1545kJ; Protein 4g; Carbohydrate 55g, of which sugars 52g; Fat 16g, of which saturates 10g; Cholesterol 440mg; Calcium 81mg; Fibre 1.1g; Sodium 400mg.

Sugar and rum sauce for fried bananas

This Caribbean-inspired dish with rum is strictly for grown-ups. Fried bananas can be incredibly sweet, but the lime juice cuts through the sweetness with delicious results.

SERVES 4

4 bananas, peeled
vanilla ice cream, to serve

FOR THE SAUCE
50g/2oz/¼ cup caster (superfine) sugar
45ml/3 tbsp rum
65g/2½oz/5 tbsp unsalted (sweet) butter
grated rind and juice of 1 lime

1 To make the sauce, place the sugar, rum, butter, grated lime rind and lime juice in a large heavy frying pan over low heat. Cook for a few minutes, stirring occasionally, until the sugar has completely dissolved.

2 Add the bananas to the pan, turning to coat them in the sauce. Cook over medium heat for 5 minutes on each side, or until the bananas are golden. Remove the pan from the heat and cut the bananas in half.

3 Serve two pieces of banana per person with a scoop of vanilla ice cream and a generous drizzle of the hot rum sauce.

Nutritional information per portion: Energy 290kcal/1213kJ; Protein 1.3g; Carbohydrate 36.4g, of which sugars 34.1g; Fat 13.7g, of which saturates 8.6g; Cholesterol 35mg; Calcium 10mg; Fibre 1.1g; Sodium 100mg.

Butterscotch sauce for apple crêpes

These wonderful dessert crêpes are enriched with sweet cider, filled with caramelized apples and drizzled with a rich, smooth butterscotch sauce which will be loved by everyone.

SERVES 4

115g/4oz/1 cup plain (all-purpose) flour
pinch of salt
2 eggs
175ml/6fl oz/3/4 cup creamy milk
120ml/4fl oz/1/2 cup sweet (hard) cider
90g/3 1/2 oz/scant 1/2 cup butter, and extra for frying
4 Braeburn apples, cored and cut into thick slices

FOR THE SAUCE

225g/8oz/1 1/3 cups light muscovado (brown) sugar
150ml/1/4 pint/2/3 cup double (heavy) cream

1 Make the crêpe batter. Sift the flour and salt into a bowl. Add the eggs and milk and beat until smooth. Stir in the cider and set aside for 30 minutes.

2 Heat a non-stick frying pan. Heat a little butter and ladle in enough batter to coat the pan thinly. Cook until all the crêpes are golden on both sides.

3 Make the filling. Heat 15g/1/2 oz/1 tbsp of the butter in a large frying pan. Add the apples to the pan. Cook until golden on both sides. Set them aside.

4 To make the sauce, add the rest of the butter to the pan. Once melted, add the muscovado sugar. When the sugar has dissolved and the mixture is bubbling, stir in the cream. Continue cooking until it forms a smooth sauce.

5 Fold each pancake into a cone. Fill with the apples and serve with the sauce.

Nutritional information per portion: Energy 799kcal/3349kJ; Protein 9g; Carbohydrate 97g, of which sugars 75g; Fat 45g, of which saturates 27g; Cholesterol 222mg; Calcium 177mg; Fibre 3.3g; Sodium 333mg.

Orange sauce for crêpes

This is one of the best-known French desserts and is easy to do at home. You can make the crêpes in advance, and then coat them in the tangy orange sauce at the last minute.

SERVES 6

115g/4oz/1 cup plain (all-purpose) flour
1.5ml/¼ tsp salt
25g/1oz/2 tbsp caster (superfine) sugar
2 eggs, lightly beaten
about 250ml/8fl oz/1 cup milk
about 60ml/4 tbsp water
30ml/2 tbsp orange flower water, Cointreau or orange liqueur
25g/1oz/2 tbsp unsalted (sweet) butter, melted, plus extra for frying

FOR THE SAUCE

75g/3oz/6 tbsp unsalted (sweet) butter
50g/2oz/¼ cup caster (superfine) sugar
grated rind and juice of 1 large orange, such as Jaffa
grated rind and juice of 1 lemon
150ml/¼ pint/⅔ cup freshly squeezed orange juice
60ml/4 tbsp Cointreau or orange liqueur, plus more for flaming (optional)
brandy, for flaming (optional)
orange segments, to decorate

1 Sift the flour, salt and sugar into a bowl. Make a well in the centre and add the eggs. Beat the eggs, gradually incorporating the flour.

2 Whisk in the milk, water and orange flower water or liqueur to make a very smooth batter. Strain into a jug (pitcher) and set aside for 20–30 minutes.

3 Heat a 18–20cm/7–8in non-stick frying pan over medium heat. If the batter has thickened, add a little water or milk to thin it. Stir the melted butter into the batter.

4 Brush the hot pan with a little melted butter and pour in about 30ml/2 tbsp of batter. Quickly coat the base with a thin layer of batter. Cook for 1 minute, or until the top has set and the base is golden. Then carefully turn over the crêpe and cook for 20–30 seconds, just to set. Transfer on to a plate.

5 Continue cooking the crêpes, stirring the batter occasionally and brushing the pan with a little more melted butter when necessary. Place a sheet of clear film (plastic wrap) or baking parchment between each crêpe as they are stacked to prevent them from sticking. (The crêpes can be prepared ahead to this point – put them in a plastic bag and chill until ready to use.)

6 To make the sauce, melt the butter in a large frying pan over medium-low heat, then stir in the sugar, orange and lemon rind and juice, the additional orange juice and the orange liqueur.

7 Place a crêpe in the pan browned side down, swirling gently to coat with the sauce. Fold it in half, then in half again to form a triangle. Continue until all the crêpes are covered with the sauce.

8 To flame, heat 30–45ml/2–3 tbsp each of orange liqueur and brandy in a small pan over medium heat. Remove from the heat, carefully ignite the liquid with a match then pour evenly over the crêpes. Top with the orange segments and serve.

Nutritional information per portion: Energy 316kcal/1323kJ; Protein 5.6g; Carbohydrate 34.2g, of which sugars 19.6g; Fat 17.2g, of which saturates 10.1g; Cholesterol 103mg; Calcium 100mg; Fibre 0.6g; Sodium 152mg.

Blueberry compote for waffles

Sweet stewed blueberries are delicious served with freshly cooked hot waffles. The compote can also be served with grilled goat's cheese, pancakes or rice pudding.

MAKES 20

25g/1oz/1 tbsp unsalted (sweet) butter, plus extra for greasing
350g/12oz/3 cups plain (all-purpose) flour
350ml/12fl oz/1½ cups water
475ml/16fl oz/2 cups double (heavy) cream

FOR THE COMPOTE

200g/7oz blueberries, fresh or frozen
15ml/1 tbsp sugar
5ml/1 tsp balsamic vinegar
pinch of ground cinnamon
pinch of ground cloves

1 To make the compote, put the blueberries into a pan, then add the sugar, vinegar, cinnamon and cloves and poach for about 5 minutes until soft and liquid.

2 Bring to the boil and cook for a further 4 minutes to reduce the liquid. Either keep the compote warm, or cool and store in the refrigerator for up to 1 month.

3 To make the waffles, melt the butter. Put the flour in a bowl and gradually beat in the water to form a smooth mixture then add the melted butter. Whisk the cream until stiff then fold into the mixture.

4 Preheat a waffle iron according to the manufacturer's instructions. Cook the waffles until golden and crispy. Serve hot with the compote.

Nutritional information per portion: Energy 189kcal/787kJ; Protein 2.12g; Carbohydrate 14.52g, of which sugars 1.18g; Fat 14.03g, of which saturates 8.62g; Cholesterol 35mg; Calcium 41mg; Fibre 0,85g; Sodium 14mg.

Spiced dark cherry sauce for rice pudding

Rice pudding topped with fruit is a classic partnership – a combination that is hard to beat for a warming dessert. Try this sauce with a slice of melon or with vanilla ice cream.

SERVES 6–8

1.5 litres/2½ pints/6¼ cups milk
1 vanilla pod (bean)
225g/8oz/1 cup short grain rice
25g/1oz/2 tbsp caster (superfine) sugar
25g/1oz/2 tbsp vanilla sugar
50g/2oz/½ cup chopped blanched almonds
250ml/8fl oz/1 cup double (heavy) cream

FOR THE SAUCE

450g/1lb fresh or bottled dark cherries, stoned (pitted), cut into quarters
90g/3½ oz/½ cup sugar
5ml/1 tsp fresh lemon juice
2 whole cloves
30ml/2 tbsp cornflour (cornstarch)

1 Pour the milk into the top of a double boiler. Slit open the vanilla pod and scrape the seeds into the milk; add the pod. Bring to the boil, then add the rice, lower the heat, cover, and cook for 2 hours, stirring occasionally, until almost all the milk is absorbed. Remove the lid for the last 10 minutes.

2 Remove from the heat and leave to cool slightly. While it is still warm, stir in the caster sugar, vanilla sugar and chopped almonds. Chill. Whip the cream until stiff and gently fold it into the cold rice pudding. Turn into a serving dish and chill.

3 To make the sauce, put the cherries in a pan with 475ml/16fl oz/2 cups water, the sugar, lemon juice and cloves.

4 Bring to the boil and cook gently, stirring, for about 20 minutes. Transfer a small amount of the cherry juice to a small bowl.

5 Add the cornflour to the juice and blend to a smooth paste. Stir the cornflour mixture into the cherries and cook for 10 minutes more, until thickened. Remove the pan from the heat and cool. Serve drizzled over the rice pudding.

Nutritional information per portion: Energy 503kcal/2107kJ; Protein 10.7g; Carbohydrate 64.4g, of which sugars 38.3g; Fat 23.6g, of which saturates 12.7g; Cholesterol 54mg; Calcium 279mg; Fibre 0.8g; Sodium 96mg.

Spiced redcurrant sauce for semolina

This is one of the simplest of all pudding sauces. This sauce can also be made with blackberries, blackcurrants or blueberries; simply omit the flour and cook to taste with the sugar.

SERVES 4

800ml/1$^1/_3$ pints/3$^1/_2$ cups milk
rind of $^1/_2$ lemon
75g/3oz/$^1/_2$ cup semolina
65g/2$^1/_2$oz/$^1/_3$ cup sugar
pinch of salt
1 egg, beaten
15g/$^1/_2$oz/1 tbsp butter
40g/1$^1/_2$oz/$^1/_3$ cup coarsely ground almonds

FOR THE SAUCE
250ml/8fl oz/1 cup redcurrant juice
1 cinnamon stick
45ml/3 tbsp potato flour
65g/2$^1/_2$oz/$^1/_3$ cup sugar, or to taste

1 Rinse out a heavy pan with cold water, pour in the milk, add the lemon rind and bring to the boil.

2 Mix together the semolina, sugar and salt and add to the boiling milk, stirring constantly. Cook over low heat, stirring, for about 5 minutes, until thickened. Discard the lemon rind.

3 Whisk the beaten egg into the mixture and cook for a few minutes more. Stir in the butter and ground almonds, and remove the pan from the heat.

4 Rinse out a 1-litre/1$^3/_4$-pint/4-cup mould with cold water and pour in the semolina mixture. Leave to cool, then chill in the refrigerator until set.

5 Meanwhile, make the spiced redcurrant sauce. Pour the redcurrant juice into a pan, add 250ml/8fl oz/1 cup water and the cinnamon and bring to the boil. Lower the heat and simmer for 30 minutes.

6 Mix the potato flour with 90ml/6 tbsp cold water to a paste in a bowl, stir into the sauce and cook, stirring constantly, until thickened. Add sugar to taste and remove from the heat.

7 To serve, turn out the pudding on to a platter and then drizzle a little of the sauce over it. Serve the remainder of the sauce in a sauceboat.

Nutritional information per portion: Energy 398kcal/1679kJ; Protein 12.9g; Carbohydrate 59.3g, of which sugars 34.1g; Fat 13.9g, of which saturates 4.9g; Cholesterol 67mg; Calcium 297mg; Fibre 1.2g; Sodium 141mg.

Spiced sugar syrup for cakes

This is a sweet and very indulgent cake. It is made deliciously moist by the unusual method of simmering the cooked slices in a spicy sugar syrup, after it has been baked.

SERVES 8

12 egg yolks
15ml/1 tbsp self-raising (self-rising) flour
5ml/1 tsp baking powder
flaked (sliced) almonds, toasted, to decorate

FOR THE SYRUP
1 litre/1¾ pints/4 cups water
500g/1¼lb/2½ cups sugar
1 large cinnamon stick
3 cloves

1 Preheat the oven to 160°C/325°F/Gas 3 and grease or line a 25cm/10in square cake tin (pan).

2 Whisk the egg yolks in a bowl until they are thick and almost white. Sift in the flour and baking powder and fold in gently.

3 Pour into the prepared tin and bake for 20 minutes, until golden. Leave the cake to cool in the tin.

4 To make the syrup, put the water, sugar, cinnamon and cloves in a wide pan. Heat gently, stirring, until the sugar has dissolved. Boil for 10 minutes over high heat to make a syrup. Reduce the heat to low.

5 Cut the cake into slices and place in the syrup. Simmer for 10 minutes, then lift them out with a slotted spoon and leave to cool. Decorate with toasted, flaked almonds.

Nutritional information per portion: Energy 344kcal/1456kJ; Protein 4.8g; Carbohydrate 66.8g, of which sugars 65.3g; Fat 8.3g, of which saturates 2.4g; Cholesterol 302mg; Calcium 71mg; Fibre 0.1g; Sodium 17mg.

Kumquat sauce for **sponge cakes**

The intense flavour of kumquats makes these dainty puddings special. Served with more kumquats in a creamy sauce, this is a dessert that is sure to please.

SERVES 8

1 pre-cooked sponge cake, cut into 8 rounds

FOR THE SAUCE

75g/3oz kumquats, thinly sliced
75g/3oz/6 tbsp caster (superfine) sugar
250ml/8fl oz/1 cup water
150ml/¼ pint/⅔ cup crème fraîche
5ml/1 tsp cornflour (cornstarch) mixed with 10ml/2 tsp water
lemon juice, to taste

1 To make the sauce, put the kumquats, sugar and water in a large pan and bring to the boil, stirring until the sugar has dissolved.

2 Simmer for a further 5 minutes. Stir in the crème fraîche and bring the mixture back to the boil, stirring frequently. Remove from the heat.

3 Whisk in the cornflour mixture. Return the pan to the heat and simmer very gently for 2 minutes, stirring constantly. Then add the lemon juice to taste.

4 Place the cakes on plates and serve with the hot sauce spooned over and around the sponges.

Nutritional information per portion: Energy 402kcal/1680kJ; Protein 3.7g; Carbohydrate 44.4g, of which sugars 33.7g; Fat 24.5g, of which saturates 15.3g; Cholesterol 109mg; Calcium 93mg; Fibre 1g; Sodium 190mg.

Rum and chocolate sauce for mousse

Happy endings are assured when slices of creamy white chocolate mousse are served with a divine dark chocolate sauce. This sauce is so versatile – it's good with fruit, ice cream or pancakes.

SERVES 4

200g/7oz white chocolate
2 eggs, separated
60ml/4 tbsp caster (superfine) sugar
300ml/$^1/_2$ pint/1$^1/_4$ cups double (heavy) cream
1 sachet powdered gelatine
150ml/$^1/_4$ pint/$^2/_3$ cup Greek (US strained plain) yogurt
10ml/2 tsp vanilla extract

FOR THE SAUCE

50g/2oz plain (semisweet) chocolate, broken into squares
30ml/2 tbsp dark rum
60ml/4 tbsp single (light) cream

1 Line a 1-litre/1$^3/_4$-pint/4-cup loaf tin (pan) with baking parchment or clear film (plastic wrap). Break the white chocolate into squares, and melt in a heatproof bowl over hot water, then remove from the heat.

2 Whisk the egg yolks and sugar in a bowl until pale and thick, then beat in the melted chocolate.

3 Heat the cream in a small pan until almost boiling, then remove from the heat. Sprinkle the powdered gelatine over, stirring until dissolved. Then pour on to the white chocolate mixture, whisking vigorously until smooth.

4 Whisk the yogurt and vanilla extract into the mixture. In a clean bowl, whisk the egg whites until stiff, then fold them into the mixture. Turn into the prepared loaf tin, level the surface and chill the mousse until set.

5 To make the sauce, melt the plain chocolate with the rum and cream in a heatproof bowl over a pan of barely simmering water, stirring occasionally, then leave to cool completely.

6 When the mousse is set, remove it from the tin with the aid of the baking parchment or clear film. Serve in thick slices with the cooled rum and chocolate sauce poured around.

Nutritional information per portion: Energy 534kcal/2221kJ; Protein 45.8g; Carbohydrate 4.5g, of which sugars 1.1g; Fat 33.4g, of which saturates 8.2g; Cholesterol 345mg; Calcium 92mg; Fibre 1.1g; Sodium 145mg.

A guide to making sauces

There is no great secret to sauces – it's simply a matter of marrying tried and tested techniques with good ingredients, and partnering the right sauce with the main food. A little know-how goes a long way, so it's worth learning the basics – when to boil or simmer, why some sauces are whisked and others stirred, and what to prepare in advance for last-minute perfection.

Flours

There is a wide range of flours and thickening agents on the market. It is important to select the right product, since the choice of flour used for a sauce will determine not only the cooking method used, but the texture and flavour of the finished sauce. These general guidelines should help remove any mystique involved.

BELOW: *from left to right: Brown flour, wholemeal flour*

BELOW: *Sauce flour*

Plain white flour

Also known as all-purpose flour, this is the standard choice for making roux-based sauces and gravies. Its fine, smooth texture combines easily with melted fat for a sauce with a roux base, so that when heated, the starch grains burst and cook, thickening the sauce liquid.

White flour usually contains 70–75 per cent of the wheatgrain. Most of the bran and wheatgerm have been removed during milling, leaving it almost white, so it is excellent for thickening white sauces. White flour is chemically bleached, making it pale in colour and therefore more suitable for white sauces than unbleached, stoneground flours.

BELOW: *Plain flour*

Self-raising, strong and soft flours

These are flours designed for specific baking uses, not for sauces, but could be used in an emergency if you run out of plain flour. Self-raising (self-rising) flour has chemical agents added during milling which react with heat to make cake mixtures rise during cooking. Strong flour, or bread flour, has a higher proportion of gluten, making it most suitable for bread making. Soft flours, or sponge flours, have a lower gluten content, and are designed for cakes, but they also make good thickeners for light and airy sauces.

Wholemeal, wheatmeal and brown flours

All of these flours contain more of the bran and wheatgerm, between 80 and 90 per cent of the grain, which gives them a nutty flavour and coarse texture, and a darker colour than white flour. Because of this, they are not usually chosen for making sauces, but if you don't mind the texture and colour, there's no reason why any of these flours should not be used for thickening sauces. The bonus is that they will add a little extra dietary fibre and nutrients to the dish.

Sauce flour

This flour has been recently introduced, and has a lower protein level than ordinary wheat flour, so that sauces made with it are less likely to go lumpy. It is designed specifically for making cooked white sauces and gravies. It is also a good choice for making low-fat sauces, since it is suitable for use in recipes made by the all-in-one, or blending method, in which no fat is used to mix the flour to a paste.

Cornflour

Also known as cornstarch, this fine maize flour is gluten-free. It is light and smooth, producing velvety-textured sauces, usually made by the blending method. For smooth results it has to be mixed to a smooth paste with a little cold liquid (a technique known as slaking) before adding hot liquid. It is widely used in Chinese sauces, and its light, slightly jellied, texture makes it particularly suitable for sweet sauces and blancmange, or light sauces for coating foods.

ABOVE: *clockwise from top left: Cornflour (cornstarch), custard powder, potato flour, arrowroot*

Potato flour

Also known as *farine de fécule*, potato flour is made from pure potato starch. It is very fine and smooth and is bright white in colour. It makes a light, clear thickener for sauces without affecting the flavour. You will need to use slightly less potato flour than ordinary plain flour for thickening. It is most suited to the blending method of sauce making, and is often used as a thickener in Chinese and Asian dishes and stir-fry sauces, so it is easily available from Asian stores.

Arrowroot

This is a white, finely ground powder made from the root of a tropical tree, which is grown in Central America. It is used as a thickening agent, in the same way as cornflour, for sauces made by the blending method. Whereas cornflour makes an opaque sauce, arrowroot clears when boiled. It is often used in sweet glazes.

Custard powder

Useful for making quick custard sauces when you're in a hurry. This is an unsweetened cornflour-based mix flavoured with vanilla. A similar result can be achieved by enriching a cornflour sauce with egg yolks and adding vanilla extract. Make up with milk by the blending method. Sweeten to taste.

Storing Flour

Store flour in a cool, dark, dry, airy place, away from steam or damp. Place the flour into a clean tin or a storage jar with a close-fitting lid, and always make sure you wash and dry the container thoroughly before refilling it. Check the use by dates, and use up the flour within the recommended pack date, or replace it. Don't add new flour to old in a storage jar – it is always best to use up the older flour first.

Once opened, plain white (all-purpose) flour can be stored under the right conditions for about six months, but wholemeal (whole-wheat) and brown flours have a higher fat content so these are best used within two months. Like all food, flour is best used while fresh – it develops off flavours, ultimately becoming rancid, when old. If stored in damp conditions, it tastes musty, so buy in small quantities.

Fats and oils

Fats and oils make sauces palatable, and improve the flavour and texture. The ones usually used in sauces are 'yellow' fats, such as butter or margarine, or oils.

RIGHT: *Ghee*

BELOW: *Clarified butter*

LEFT: *Concentrated butter*

USING FATS AND OILS

Many fats and oils are combined with white flour in sauces, for example in a roux, a cooked paste, or in beurre manié, a raw paste. Heating flour with fat allows liquid to be incorporated into the sauce without forming lumps. The classic emulsified sauces, such as hollandaise or mayonnaise, use either melted butter or liquid oils, and are beaten with eggs until combined and thickened in an creamy emulsion. The same principle is used in reduced sauces, such as beurre blanc, or in oil-based salad dressings such as vinaigrette, where the fat is whisked into a reduced or well-flavoured liquid base to make a smooth emulsion.

In salsas and purées, oil is added for flavour by stirring into, or drizzling over, the other ingredients.

LEFT: *Lactic unsalted butter (left) and sweetcream salted butter*

TYPES OF FAT

Saturated fats are solid at room temperature, and are the ones that can raise cholesterol levels in the blood. Polyunsaturated fats can help lower cholesterol levels; mono-unsaturated fats, which are beneficial in regulating cholesterol levels, are liquid but can be made solid by a process known as hydrogenation. This is the process used to make margarines and spreads.

Butter

A natural product made by churning cream, butter has an 80 per cent fat content, which is saturated fat. Butter is made in two basic types, sweetcream and lactic, and both are available salted, lightly salted or unsalted (sweet). The choice will depend largely on flavour, according to whether you are making a sweet or savoury sauce. There are other alternatives, however. Clarified butter, ghee or concentrated butters, which can be made at home, will withstand higher temperatures than untreated butter, and will not burn as easily.

Margarine

Soft (tub) margarines, made from a blend of vegetable oils and/or animal oils, have a soft, spreadable texture. Hard (packet) margarines have a firmer texture and are made from animal and vegetable fats. Both types have the same fat content as butter, and can be used as a direct substitute for butter in making sweet and savoury sauces. As the flavour is inferior to butter, margarines are best chosen for more robustly flavoured sauces where their own flavour will not be as noticeable.

Spreads

The wide choice of different spreads on the market is confusing to say the least, but as a rough guide, unless they are labelled low-fat, or very low-fat, they are generally suitable for sauce-making. After that, choice is very much a matter of personal taste and preference.

Polyunsaturated vegetable oil spreads: Products described in this way are made either from a single vegetable oil or sunflower oil alone, or from a blend of different vegetable oils. They vary in fat content from 61 to 79 per cent.

Monounsaturated vegetable oil spreads: Made from olive oil or rapeseed (canola) oil, these vary in fat content from 60 to 75 per cent.

Dairy spreads: These contain cream or buttermilk to retain a buttery flavour and smooth texture, while providing a lower-fat alternative to butter. The fat content varies between 61 and 75 per cent.

Reduced-fat spreads: These products are either made from vegetable oils alone or may also contain some dairy or animal fat. Their fat content is between 50 and 60 per cent.

Low-fat spreads and very low-fat spreads: These spreads, popular with the weight-conscious, contain less than 40 per cent fat, and are often as low as 25 per cent. They are not recommended for cooking, although they can be added to all-in-one method sauces.

Storing fat

All solid fats should be stored in the refrigerator, below 4°C/39°F. They should be covered or closely wrapped to protect them from light and air. Keep them away from strong-smelling foods as they can absorb other flavours easily. (The section used for storing butter in most refrigerators is in the door, and is not quite so cold as other parts, so the butter should not become too hard.) Oils tend to solidify at low temperatures, so are best kept in a cool cupboard with a temperature of 4–12°C/39–54°F.

Making a Flavoured Butter

Flavoured butters can make good accompaniments for both sweet and savoury dishes. Herb and garlic butters are delicious with fish or grilled (broiled) meat, while sweet-flavoured butters can go well with steamed puddings.

1 Put 115g/4oz/1/2 cup unsalted butter (sweet) butter in a large bowl and beat the butter with a wooden spoon or an electric beater until soft.

2 Add 30–60ml/2–4 tbsp chopped fresh herbs and season with salt, pepper and a dash of lemon juice. Beat the mixture until combined.

3 Transfer the butter mixture to a piece of baking parchment and shape into a roll. Wrap and chill. Cut into slices to serve.

For more tips and ideas on making flavoured butters, see page 213.

ABOVE: *Polyunsaturated spread* **ABOVE:** *Olive spread* **ABOVE:** *Dairy spread* **ABOVE:** *Reduced-fat spread*

TYPES OF OILS

These fats are liquid at room temperature. They are used in emulsion sauces, such as mayonnaise or salad dressings, usually balanced with vinegar or other acids, such as citrus juices. However, they can also be used as a direct replacement for butter or hard fats in roux or similar flour-thickened sauces, with good results. With the exception of coconut oil and palm oil, they are mostly rich in unsaturated fat, which helps reduce cholesterol levels. The choice of individual oils for a particular sauce depends largely on flavour and personal taste.

Groundnut (peanut) oil: Made from peanuts, this is usually used where a mild flavour is required.

Sesame seed oil: Usually used for flavouring Asian sauces at the end of cooking, as it has an intense, rich flavour and burns easily when heated. However, it can be heated with care, or mixed half and half with another oil, such as groundnut, if necessary.

Soya oil: A mild-flavoured oil which will withstand high temperatures, this keeps well and is economical to use.

Sunflower oil: A little more expensive to use than soya oil, this versatile, light-flavoured oil is good for sauces or dressings, as it does not mask other flavours.

Nut oils: Walnut and hazelnut oils are the most commonly used nut oils for dressings, lending their rich, distinctive flavours to salads. Use in moderation, perhaps combined with a milder oil, as the flavours can be strong. Almond oil is a pale and delicate oil that is mainly used in confectionery and desserts.

BELOW: *from left: Groundnut oil, sunflower oil, soya oil, sesame oil, walnut oil*

Olive oils

The characteristics and quality of olive oils vary and depend on variety, growing region and method of production. Many are blended, but the best-quality oils are produced on individual estates. For most sauces, including mayonnaise, it's best to choose virgin or pure olive oil, and keep the more expensive extra virgin ones for salad dressings, or for drizzling directly over foods. It is more economical to buy olive oils in larger quantities.

Extra virgin first pressed or cold pressed olive oils: These oils are made from the first pressing of the olives, with no extra treatment, such as heat or blending. By law, these oils never have more than 1 per cent acidity, ensuring a fine flavour. They have a distinctive flavour and pungent aroma. They are usually a deep green colour and are sometimes cloudy, although both of these factors vary according to the area where the oil was produced.

Virgin olive oil: This is also cold pressed and unrefined, but has a higher acidity content than extra virgin oil, with a maximum level of 1 to 1.5 per cent.

Pure olive oil: This comes from the third or fourth pressing of the olives, and is usually blended. It has a maximum acid content of 2 per cent. It is mild, rather than overpowering, and therefore widely used in cooking.

Light olive oil: This is a product created during the last pressing of the fruit. The term 'light' refers to the clear colour and delicate flavour.

Store cupboard

A well-stocked pantry makes every cook's life a lot easier, and when it comes to sauce making, it really makes sense. Just by keeping a few basic ingredients in stock, you will always be able to whip up an impromptu sauce when the occasion demands, transforming a simple dish into something special.

Stock cubes and powders

There is a wide choice of commercial stock (bouillon) cubes and powders, and these vary in flavour and quality. Good-quality products make adequate substitutes for fresh stock, and certainly they are very convenient to use. However, some tend to be quite salty, so allow for this when adding other seasonings. Follow the pack directions for quantities to use. Generally speaking, it is worth paying a little more for good-quality stock cubes or powder, and it is worth choosing one that is made with natural ingredients for a more natural flavour.

Many supermarkets also now sell cartons of basic ready-made fresh stocks on the chilled foods counter, including beef, chicken, fish and vegetable stock. These are a good substitute for home-made if you're short of time.

Canned consommé makes an excellent substitute for a good brown stock in rich savoury sauces, so is well worth keeping handy in the store cupboard. If you need a light stock, the colour of consommé may be too dark to use, but brands do vary widely.

BELOW: *Stock cubes and powder*

Canned tomatoes and boiled sauces

Since many of the plum tomatoes we buy out of season are lacking in flavour, it's a safer bet to go for good-quality canned tomatoes in recipes, either whole or chopped. The best are from Italy, so check the label. Polpa di pomodoro are finely chopped or crushed. Avoid canned tomatoes with added herbs or spices, as it is best to add herbs fresh.

BELOW: *Consommé*

BELOW: *clockwise from left: Passata, sugocasa, whole plum tomatoes, tomato purée, chopped tomatoes in tomato juice*

Crushed or creamed tomatoes: Sold as sugocasa, polpa and passata (bottled strained tomatoes), and usually packed in convenient jars, long-life packs or bottles, these products are invaluable for sauces. Sugocasa and polpa both have a chunky texture, while passata is sieved to a creamy and smooth purée.

Tomato purée (paste): This is concentrated, cooked tomato pulp in a strong, thick paste, and is sold in tubes or cans. The strength of different brands varies, so use with care or the flavour can overpower a sauce. Sun-dried tomato paste has a sweet, rich flavour, and is milder than ordinary tomato purée. Keep in the refrigerator once opened.

Tomato ketchup: This sweet, vinegary, and slightly spicy sauce is typically served with sausages, burgers and chips (French fries). It is also extremely useful as a flavouring ingredient and can be added to soups, sauces and dressings.

Making Tomato Ketchup

Chop 2.75g/6lb tomatoes into quarters and put in a pan with 25g/1oz salt and 600ml/1 pint/ 2/1/2 cups vinegar. Simmer until the tomatoes are soft, then strain through a muslin (cheesecloth). Return the pureé to the pan and add 225g/ 8oz sugar and simmer until it thickens. Add 2.5ml/1/2 tsp each of allspice, ground cloves, cinnamon and cayenne. Pour into bottles.

Commercial sauces

The huge range of commercially made flavouring sauces or condiments now available is a boon to the creative cook. The following are some of the most useful to keep in your store cupboard.

Hot pepper sauces: Widely used in West Indian and South American cooking, there are many versions of pepper sauce, the most famous being Tabasco. Use with caution, as they can be fiery hot. These sauces will pep up almost any savoury sauce, marinade or dressing.

Mustards: Ready-made mustards are a blend of ground mustard seeds with flour and salt, often with wine, herbs and other spices. Dijon is often used for classic French sauces and for dressings such as vinaigrette and mayonnaise – it also helps to stabilize the emulsion. Yellow English (hot) mustard is a good choice to give bite to cheese sauce or to flavour rich gravies for meat. Milder German mustard is good for a barbecue sauce to serve with chops or sausages. Mild, creamy American mustard is squeezed on hotdogs or burgers. Wholegrain mustard gives a pleasant texture to creamy savoury sauces and dressings.

Oyster sauce: A thicker-textured sauce made with the extract of real oysters, this adds a delicious sweet-savoury flavour to dishes.

LEFT: *top row from left: Oyster sauce, soy sauce, Worcestershire sauce, fish sauce, hot pepper sauce; bottom row: Red pesto, green pesto, English mustard*

Pesto: Commercially made pesto is sold in jars, either the traditional green basil pesto, or a red pesto made from sun-dried tomatoes. Use it just as it is as a replacement for fresh pesto sauce to stir into pasta, pepped up with a little freshly grated Parmesan cheese or an extra drizzle of olive oil. You can also add it by the spoonful to enrich and enhance the flavour of tomato sauces, salsas and dressings. Once the jar is opened, this type of product should be treated as fresh and stored in the refrigerator.

Soy sauce: Although this is traditionally used for Chinese and Japanese foods, there is no need to limit its use to Asian dishes. Use it to flavour and colour all kinds of savoury sauces, marinades and dressings. Light soy sauce is good in light, sweet-and-sour or stir-fry sauces for fish or vegetables, and the richer, sweeter dark soy sauce is best with rich meat sauces, such as satays, or for barbecue sauces.

Thai fish sauce or nam pla: This is a classic Thai sauce made from fermented fish. It has a pungent flavour and is best in cooked sauces. It adds a richness to sauces for both meat and fish. Once opened it should be kept in a cool, dark place where it will keep for up to a year.

Worcestershire sauce: This classic English sauce has its origins in India. Its spicy, mellowed, but piquant, flavour enhances savoury sauces, marinades and dressings of any type. It is often used to bring out meaty flavours in gravies and long-cooked casserole sauces.

Vinegars

These aromatic vinegars are based on malt, wine, beer, cider, rice wine and sugar, and are often used to enhance flavour in sauces or as emulsifiers. Dark, long-matured sherry or balsamic vinegars have intense, powerful flavours and you may only need a few drops. They are often used in dressings and marinades.

ABOVE: *Red and white wine vinegars and fruit vinegars*

Coconut Milk and Cream

Popular ingredients in Asian cuisine, coconut milk and cream are used widely in dishes based on spicy and curried sauces. They can be used rather like dairy products, for thickening, enriching and flavouring.

Coconut milk: This is available in cans and long-life packs. It is similar in thickness to single (light) cream.

Coconut cream: This has the thickness of double (heavy) cream.

RIGHT: *from left, coconut cream, coconut milk, creamed coconut blocks*

Creamed coconut is solid and white; it is sold in solid blocks, so you can cut off just the amount you need and melt it into sauces or hot water.

Dairy products

The number of sauces based on dairy products is vast, so it is worth taking the time to understand the many different products available. You may be aiming for a rich and creamy sauce, or perhaps you would prefer a lighter, healthier alternative. The following descriptions of the different types should help.

Milk

The choice of milk for sauces depends upon the richness desired – for a rich flavour and creamy texture, choose whole milk or full-fat milk, but if you're watching fat levels and looking for a lighter sauce, go for skimmed or semi-skimmed (low-fat).

Pasteurized: Most milk has been pasteurized, that is heat-treated, to destroy harmful bacteria. This should keep for up to 5 days in a refrigerator.

Homogenized: This has been processed to distribute the fat globules evenly throughout the milk, instead of rising to the surface as cream. It has the same keeping quality as ordinary milk.

Sterilized: This is homogenized, bottled and then heat-treated for 20 minutes, so that it keeps without refrigeration until opened.

UHT: This milk is homogenized then heat-treated to high temperatures for just 1–2 seconds. It has a slightly caramelized flavour, but is useful as a store-cupboard standby as it keeps unopened for up to three months without refrigeration.

Condensed: This sweetened or unsweetened milk is canned. It has been boiled until reduced and concentrated. It is very rich and the sweetened type is very sweet, but useful for rich dessert sauces.

Evaporated: Unsweetened milk that has had some of the water removed by evaporation, this milk has a concentrated flavour and is slightly caramelized. There are also lighter-fat versions available. It is available either in cans or long-life packs.

Goat's milk: Many people who are allergic to cow's milk can tolerate goat's milk, which is now widely available and can be used as a direct substitute for ordinary milk in cooking. It has a similar flavour, although it is slightly sharper, and is more digestible.

Cream

All kinds of creams can be used to enrich and thicken both sweet and savoury sauces, both hot and cold. The fat content of cream depends on the amount of butterfat it contains.

Single (light) cream: This cream has a fat content of just 18 per cent, which is too low for whipping. It will not withstand boiling, but can be stirred into sauces at the end of cooking to enrich the flavour.

Fat Levels in Milk

- Channel Islands (breakfast milk): 5–8 per cent fat
- Full-fat (whole): 4 per cent fat
- Semi-skimmed (low-fat): 1.7 per cent fat
- Skimmed: 0.1 per cent fat

BELOW, *from left: Skimmed milk, semi-skimmed milk, full-fat milk, Channel Islands milk, evaporated milk, and condensed milk*

Sour cream: In fact, this is really single (light) cream with an added souring culture, which sharpens the flavour and thickens the texture.

Double (heavy) cream: The fat content of double cream is 48 per cent. The cream almost doubles in bulk when whipped. It is especially good in hot sauces, because it can withstand boiling.

Whipping cream: This cream contains sufficient butterfat to trap air bubbles and increase volume. It is also used as a less rich alternative to double cream in sauces. This has 35 per cent fat, and whips up to a light texture, or can be stirred, unwhipped, into hot sauces after cooking without curdling.

BELOW: *clockwise from left: Single cream, whipping cream and double cream*

Crème fraîche

This has a mild, tangy flavour similar to that of sour cream, which makes it great for using in both sweet and savoury sauces and dressings. With a fat content of around 40 per cent, it is more stable than sour cream when heated. You can also buy a half-fat version, which can be successfully added to hot sauces. Crème fraîche can be used to enrich soups, casseroles and dips.

BELOW: *Low-fat yogurt*

LEFT: *Greek yogurt*

Stabilizing Yogurt for Sauces

To prevent yogurt splitting in cooked sauces, allow 5ml/1 tsp cornflour (cornstarch) to each 150ml/$^{1}/_{4}$ pint/$^{2}/_{3}$ cup yogurt. Blend the cornflour and a little yogurt to a smooth paste before adding the rest. Add to the sauce and cook following the recipe.

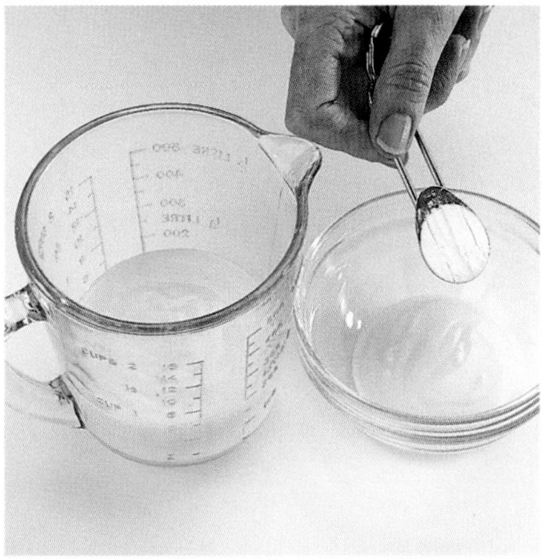

Yogurt

Products such as yogurt and other lower-fat dairy products like fromage frais, make excellent lighter replacements for cream in many sauces, savoury or sweet. In cooking, yogurt can be stabilized with cornflour (cornstarch).

Greek (US strained plain) yogurt: This may be made from either cow's or sheep's milk. It is richer in flavour and texture than most yogurts, but still only has a fat content of around 8–10 per cent, so it makes a light substitute for cream in sauces.

Low-fat yogurt: Semi-skimmed (low-fat) or skimmed milk are used to make low-fat yogurt. Both types are quite sharp and tangy, which can be refreshing in light sauces. Low-fat yogurt is also used as a base for many dips and dressings.

ABOVE: *clockwise from top: Parmesan, mascarpone, ricotta, Cheddar and Gruyère*

Eggs

As a general rule, medium (US large) eggs are the size to use for recipes, unless the recipe states otherwise, but you may find it useful to have small (US medium) eggs for using to enrich or thicken modest quantities of sauces. The freshness of supermarket eggs is easily checked, as most are individually marked with a date stamp on their shells. Fresh eggs should store well for 2 weeks, providing that the shell is not damaged or dirty. Egg shells are porous, so they are best stored at the bottom of the refrigerator away from strong-smelling foods. As a general rule, before use, eggs should be left at room temperature for 30 minutes.

Because of the slight risk of contamination in raw eggs, it is recommended that pregnant women, young children, elderly people or anyone weakened by chronic illness should avoid eating uncooked eggs.

LEFT: *Hen's eggs range in colour, from white to light brown or dark tan.*

Cheeses

Most cheese is made from cow's milk but there are also cheeses made from goat's milk, sheep's milk and water buffalo milk. Many hard cheeses can be grated and melted into sauces.

Strong, hard cheeses: Mature (sharp) cheeses such as Cheddar, Gruyère and Parmesan will grate easily and melt into hot sauces. Their fine flavour complements pasta sauces or a creamy white sauce to pour over vegetables. Always grate these cheeses freshly as you need them. Once cheese is added to a sauce, heat it gently without boiling, or it will overcook and become stringy.

Soft, fresh cheeses: Those of a creamier consistency such as ricotta or mascarpone are used to enrich sauces and dips, from tomato sauces to fruit purées or custards. Ricotta is light and mild, and makes a good base for dips. Mascarpone is rich, creamy and high in fat, and can be used in the same way as thick cream.

Sauce-making equipment

Making sauces requires very little in the way of specialist items, but a carefully selected set of basic equipment will help make tasks such as boiling, whisking and straining much easier. You may even find that most of these items are already in your kitchen. Shop around for those you still need, as quality varies enormously.

Pans

The rule here is to choose the right pan for the job, which means that your pans do not necessarily have to be a matching set. Some pans may be suitable for more than one task, but you will need a variety of sizes and types. Look for solid, heavy pans that are stable when empty, and have tight-fitting lids and firmly riveted handles. The best pans are stainless steel, with a core of copper and silver alloy in the base. Look for strong handles that do not conduct heat well and reinforced rims designed to pour cleanly. Non-stick coatings do not last as long as stainless steel. All-metal pans, which can be used in the oven as well as on the stove, are useful if you have a large oven. Buying good-quality pans is an investment, as they will last for years, but cheap, thin pans will not only wear out quickly, but also conduct heat unevenly and cause burnt spots. The following examples will cover most culinary requirements.

Milk pan: A high pan with a lip.

Three pans with lids: These range in size from about 1 litre/1$^3/_4$ pints/4 cups to 7 litres/12$^1/_3$ pints/30 cups. They should be deep and straight-sided to minimize the amount of evaporation.

Sauté pan: A deep pan with straight sides.

ABOVE: *Double boiler and heatproof bowl placed over pan*

Double boiler: A useful pan for making delicate creams and custards, and melting ingredients such as chocolate. If you don't have one, you can improvise by placing a heatproof bowl over a pan of gently boiling or simmering water.

RIGHT: *clockwise from left: Enamelled, anodized aluminium and copper pans*

Materials for pans

Stainless steel: This is attractive and hard-wearing, and providing the pans have a thick base with aluminium or copper, they will conduct heat evenly and efficiently.

Anodized aluminium: Light and easy to clean, this conducts the heat well and does not corrode. The metal reacts when in contact with acid and alkaline, so food should not be left to stand for too long in these pans.

Copper: These pans are expensive but conduct heat very efficiently and are attractive and durable. Choose pans with a stainless-steel lining, which is harder-wearing than tin.

Enamelled cast iron: This is heavy, but conducts the heat well, evenly and slowly. These pans retain the heat for a long time, and are hard-wearing and durable.

Wooden spoons

A good assortment of wooden spoons is essential, and it is a good idea to keep them for individual uses. You might reserve one for spicy sauces, one for creams and custards, and so on; then there is no risk of flavour transfer. A good selection includes a wooden spoon, a wooden corner spoon with an edge to reach into the rims of pans, and a flat-edged wooden spatula.

Whisks

Balloon whisks and spiral sauce whisks are efficient for blending or whisking. It is useful to have two different sizes.

Ladles

Available in various sizes, ladles are very useful for spooning and pouring sauces over foods. Some smaller ones have a useful lip for more precise pouring. Stainless-steel ladles are the best. A slotted stainless-steel draining spoon is invaluable for skimming and removing small pieces of ingredients from sauces.

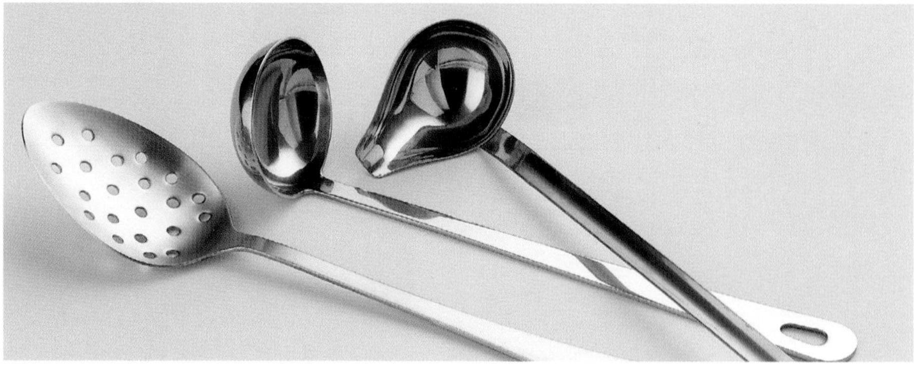

ABOVE: *from left: Draining spoon, ladles with variable cup shapes*

BELOW: *Spiral sauce whisks, balloon whisk and a selection of wooden spoons*

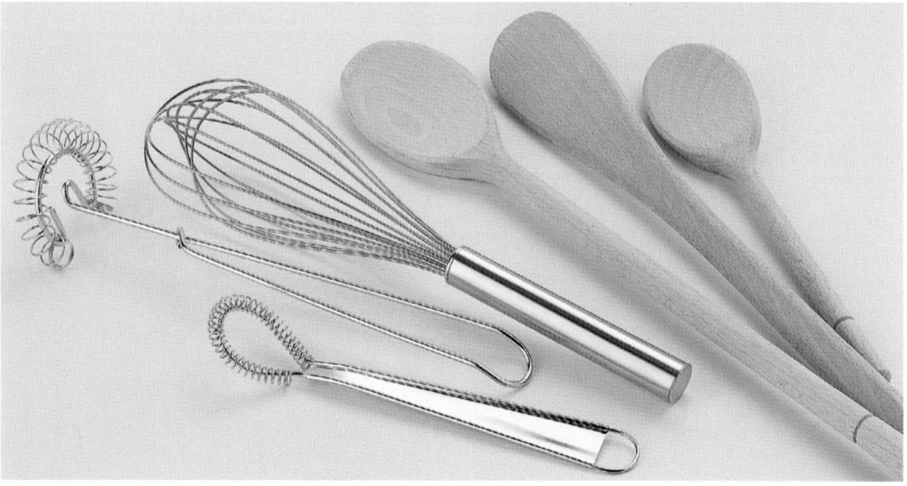

BELOW: *Measuring jug and a set of measuring spoons*

Measuring jugs

Choose a solid jug (pitcher) marked with standard measurements. Heatproof glass is ideal, as it is easy to see the liquid level and can take boiling liquids, yet the handle remains cool as it is a poor heat conductor. Stainless-steel jugs are attractive and hard-wearing.

Measuring spoons

A set of measuring spoons, either imperial or metric (select the type to correspond to the instructions you prefer to follow) is essential for accurately measuring the small amounts of sauce ingredients. Ordinary table cutlery varies widely in capacity and should not be used for measuring. Spoon measurements given in recipes are always level.

Sieve and chinois

A fine-meshed stainless-steel sieve (strainer) is essential for sauce making; look for a double-mesh, hard-wearing sieve. It can also be very useful to have a chinois, a cone-shaped sieve that is used for straining and puréeing a range of ingredients.

Electrical equipment

Although not essential for making sauces, a blender, food processor, hand blender or whisk can take much of the hard work out of many sauces and dressings. A food processor is brilliant for chopping and slicing. Hand-held electric blenders are perhaps more versatile and convenient than larger machines for sauces, as they can be used to blend or purée mixtures in a pan or jug (pitcher), and are easy to clean by simply swishing in hot soapy water after use. A hand-held electric whisk is also useful for quick beating and whisking – especially for foamy egg sauces or for whipping up creamy mixtures.

RIGHT: *Hand blender*

Sterilizing and storing

Many sauces based on flour, cheese or vegetables will keep for at least two weeks. Store in a sterilized glass jar. Jars can be boiled on top of the stove or heated in the oven to sterilize.

- Stove-top sterilizing calls for a large deep pan with a wide bottom.
- For oven sterilizing, the jars are arranged on a level roasting pan or baking tray (so the jars do not slide about), and have at least a shallow rim to prevent them from sliding off when lifted.
- Special tongs are available for lifting hot jars.
- Filling jars is easy using a wide-topped jam funnel and a small ladle or small heatproof jug.

Storing fresh sauces

A wide variety of fresh sauces can be prepared ahead and chilled or frozen. White sauces, tomato-based sauces and wine sauces are all great freezer candidates: make a big batch and freeze portions ready for thawing and reheating in the microwave.

- Airtight plastic freezer containers are ideal for chilling or freezing. Remember to allow a little headspace rather than filling the container to the brim.

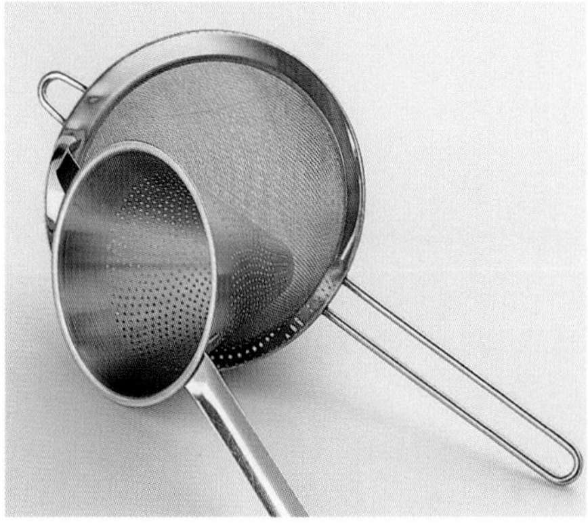

ABOVE: *from left: Chinois and sieve*

- Foil freezer bags are brilliant for sauces. They have a gusset and base, so they stand up during filling, and the top folds over to seal.
- Alternatively, supporting a freezer bag in a freezerproof bowl or jug to fill and freeze it is a good idea. When the sauce is solid, lift the bag out of the container and place in the freezer for long-term storage.

BELOW: *Hand-held electric whisk*

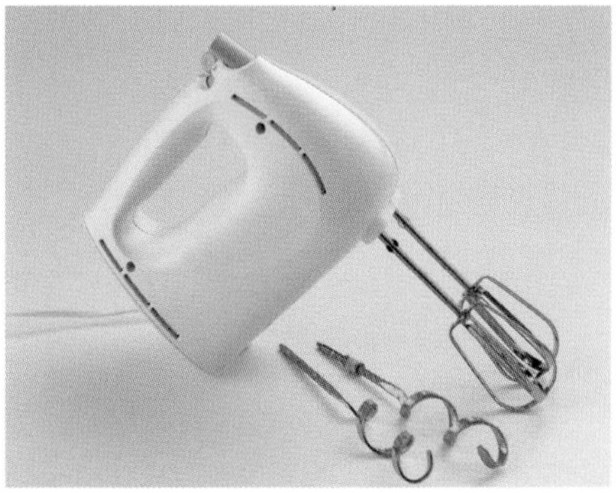

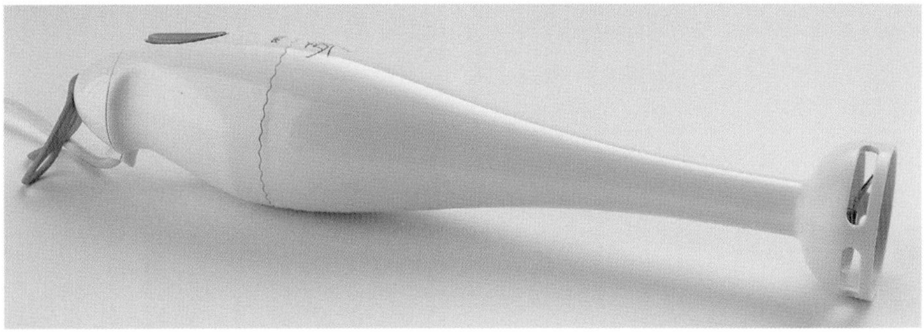

Basic stocks

Home-made stock is rich in flavour and is a wonderfully versatile ingredient that can be used to make all kinds of sauces. Commercial stock cubes and bouillon powder won't match the flavour, but can be useful for enriching a stock.
Each recipe makes about 1 litre/ $1^3/_4$ pints/4 cups.

Beef stock

675g/$1^1/_2$lb shin (shank) of beef, diced
1 large onion, chopped
1 large carrot, chopped
1 celery stick, chopped
bouquet garni
6 black peppercorns
2.5ml/$^1/_2$ tsp sea salt
1.75 litres/3 pints/$7^1/_2$ cups water

1 Place all the ingredients in a large pan and slowly bring to the boil.

2 Cover the pan and simmer very gently for 4 hours, skimming occasionally to remove scum. Strain the stock and cool.

Fish stock

1kg/$2^1/_4$lb white fish bones and trimmings
1 large onion, sliced
1 large carrot, sliced
1 celery stick, sliced
bouquet garni
6 white peppercorns
2.5ml/$^1/_2$ tsp sea salt
150ml/$^1/_4$ pint/$^2/_3$ cup dry white wine
1 litre/$1^3/_4$ pints/4 cups water

1 Place the ingredients in a pan and bring to the boil.

2 Skim any scum from the surface, cover the pan and simmer for 20 minutes. Strain and allow to cool.

Chicken stock

1 chicken carcass
chicken giblets
1 leek, chopped
1 celery stick, chopped
bouquet garni
5ml/1 tsp white peppercorns
2.5ml/$^1/_2$ tsp sea salt
1.75 litres/3 pints/$7^1/_2$ cups water

1 Break up the chicken carcass, and place it in a large pan with a lid. Then add the remaining ingredients. Boil.

2 Reduce the heat, cover and simmer for $2^1/_2$ hours, skimming off scum occasionally with a large spoon. Strain the stock into a large bowl and leave to cool.

Making a bouquet garni

A traditional bouquet garni usually contains a bay leaf, a sprig of thyme and a few sprigs of parsley, but this can be varied according to taste, and to suit the dish you are making. Other vegetables or herbs you may like to include are a piece of celery for poultry dishes; a rosemary sprig for beef or lamb; a piece of fennel or leek, or a strip of lemon rind for fish dishes.

Tie all the herbs together firmly with a piece of fine cotton string, so the bundle is easy to remove from the stock after cooking.

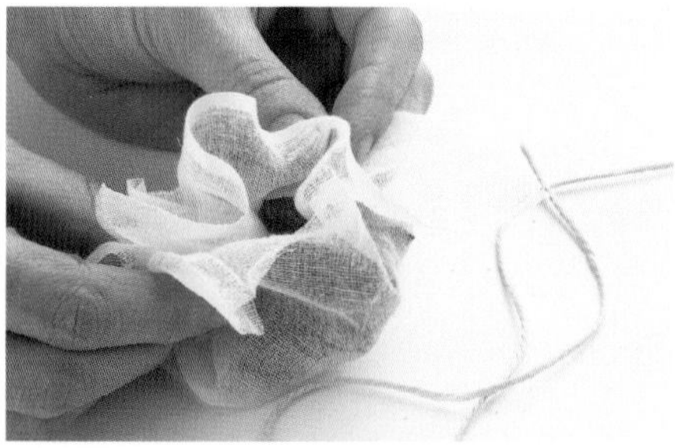

Alternatively, tie the herbs in a clean muslin (cheesecloth) cut into a square shape. Leave a long length of the string to tie to the pan handle.

Vegetable stock

500g/1¼lb chopped mixed vegetables, such as onions, carrots, celery, leeks
bouquet garni
6 black peppercorns
2.5ml/½ tsp sea salt
1 litre/1¾ pints/4 cups water

1 Place all the ingredients in a large pan and slowly bring to the boil.

2 Skim any scum from the surface, then reduce the heat and cover. Simmer gently for 30 minutes. Strain the stock and cool before chilling.

Keeping stock clear

For a clear soup it is important to keep the stock clear; avoid boiling the stock but cook it very gently, and skim the top from time to time.

1 Trim any fat from the meat or bones before adding to the pan, as it will affect the clarity of the stock.

2 Keep the heat at a low simmer, and skim off any scum as it gathers on the surface during cooking. Most vegetables can be added to stock for flavour, but potatoes tend to break down and make the stock cloudy so it's best to avoid these.

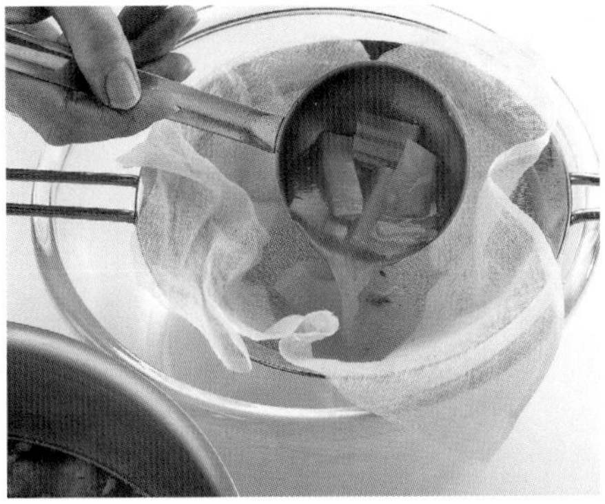

3 Strain the stock through a sieve (strainer) lined with muslin (cheesecloth), and avoid pressing the solids, as this may spoil the clarity.

Removing fat from stock

Excess fat should be removed to improve the look and taste; it also helps keep the stock clear.

1 Let the stock stand until the fat surfaces, then skim off the fat with a large, shallow spoon. To absorb more grease, blot the surface with several layers of kitchen paper.

2 Drop in a few ice cubes. The fat will set around the ice so it can be simply spooned off. Alternatively, cool then chill until the fat layer rises to the surface and sets. Then the fat can simply be lifted off. Use a large spoon to remove the solidified fat.

How to store stock

Stock will keep for a week in the refrigerator or freezes well.

1 To freeze, pour into airtight containers, allowing 2.5cm/1in headspace for expansion, then seal and freeze for up to 3 months.

2 To freeze stock in convenient portions to add to sauces, pour into ice cube trays for freezing.

Stock-making tips

- Do not salt stock: season later.
- For a brown stock from beef bones, roast the bones for 40 minutes. Add vegetables half-way through. Deglaze the pan with water and simmer.
- For concentrated stock, simmer until reduced and syrupy enough to coat a spoon. It will set to a solid jelly that will richly flavour sauces.

Flour-based sauces

The standard way to adjust the consistency of a sauce is to thicken it with a flour. The three basic methods are roux, blending, or all-in-one.

Many of the classic white sauces are based on a 'roux' – a cooked mixture of flour and fat. The most basic white sauce uses milk, but by varying the liquid used, other white sauces can be made. For a classic béchamel sauce, the milk is flavoured with vegetables and herbs. For velouté sauce, the milk is replaced with stock, giving it a more opaque appearance, which may be enriched with cream.

Roux method

When making a roux, stir the paste over the whole pan base, and add the liquid gradually; heating the liquid first helps to avoid lumps. You can adjust the amount of flour and butter to create different consistencies. A pouring sauce is poured over foods when serving. The slightly thicker coating sauce is used to make a smooth covering for fish or vegetables.

For a pouring consistency:

15g/$^1/_2$ oz/1 tbsp butter
15g/$^1/_2$ oz/2 tbsp plain (all-purpose) flour
300ml/$^1/_2$ pint/1$^1/_4$ cups liquid

For a coating consistency:

25g/1oz/2 tbsp butter
25g/1oz/$^1/_4$ cup plain (all-purpose) flour
300ml/$^1/_2$ pint/1$^1/_4$ cups liquid

1 To make the roux, melt the butter in a pan, then add the flour. Cook on low heat and stir for 1–2 minutes.

2 Allow the roux to bubble until it resembles honeycomb in texture but does not brown.

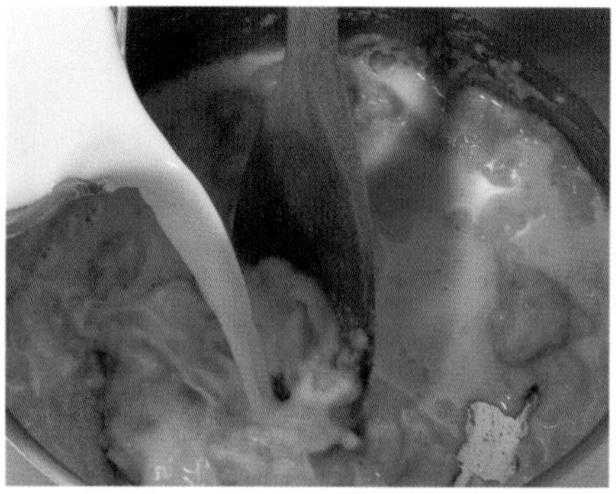

3 Off the heat, gradually stir the liquid into the roux, which may be either hot or cold. Return to the heat and stir until boiling. Reduce the heat and simmer, stirring constantly, for 2 minutes, until the sauce is thickened and smooth.

Roux Variations

Béchamel Coating Sauce: chop 1 onion, 1 carrot and 1 celery stick and place in a pan with a bouquet garni, 6 black peppercorns and a pinch of freshly grated nutmeg. Add 300ml/$^1/_2$ pint/1$^1/_4$ cups milk and boil. Strain the milk and gradually add to the prepared roux and gently heat, stirring constantly until thickened.
Velouté Pouring Sauce: in a pan bring 300ml/$^1/_2$ pint/1$^1/_4$ cups stock to the boil. Gradually add to the prepared roux, stirring constantly. Simmer until reduced by one quarter. Skim the surface removing any scum, then strain. Stir in 30ml/2 tbsp single (light) cream just before serving.

Blending method

Blending-method sauces are usually made with cornflour (cornstarch), arrowroot, potato flour or sauce flour. Cornflour and sauce flour make light, glossy sauces that are good for freezing. If you need a crystal-clear result for glazing, use arrowroot or potato flour. The liquid may be milk, stock, fruit juice or syrup from canned or poached fruit. As a guide, you will need about 20g/$^3/_4$oz/3 tbsp cornflour or sauce flour to thicken 300ml/$^1/_2$ pint/1$^1/_4$ cups liquid to a pouring consistency. Arrowroot or potato flour are slightly stronger, so use approximately 15g/$^1/_2$oz to 300ml/$^1/_2$ pint/1$^1/_4$ cups liquid to obtain the same consistency.

1 Place the cornflour in a large bowl and add just enough liquid and mix with a spoon to make a smooth, thin white paste. Heat the remaining liquid in a pan until almost boiling.

2 Pour a little hot liquid on to the blended mixture, stirring. Pour the mixture back into the pan, whisking, to avoid lumps. Return to the heat and stir until boiling, then simmer gently for 2 minutes, stirring until thickened and smooth.

All-in-one method

This uses the same ingredients and proportions as the roux method, but the liquid must be cold. Place the flour, butter and liquid in a pan and whisk over medium heat until boiling. Stir for 2 minutes, until thickened and smooth.

Using an egg yolk liaison

This is a way to lightly thicken milk, stock, cream or reduced liquids. It is good for enriching savoury white or velouté sauces. Two egg yolks enrich and thicken about 300ml/$^1/_2$ pint/ $1^1/_4$ cups liquid. A mixture of egg yolk and cream has the same effect: add it off the heat to avoid curdling.

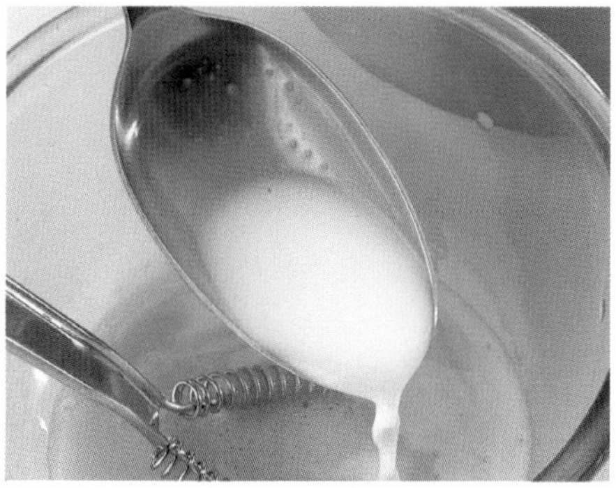

Stir 30ml/2 tbsp hot liquid or sauce into two yolks in a bowl. Return it to the rest of the sauce. Heat gently, stirring, without boiling.

Adding Flavourings to Flour-based Sauces

The following variations add flavour to a basic sauce.

- To infuse flavours into milk, stock or other liquids before using in sauces such as béchamel, pour the liquid into a pan and add thin slices or dice of onion, carrot and celery, a bouquet garni, peppercorns or a mace blade. Bring the liquid slowly to the boil, then remove the pan from the heat. Cover and leave to stand for about 10 minutes. Strain the milk to remove the flavourings before use.
- Stir 50g/2oz/$^2/_3$ cup grated Cheddar or other strong cheese into a basic white sauce with 5ml/1 tsp wholegrain mustard and a generous dash of Worcestershire sauce.
- Wine livens up the flavour of most stock-based sauces – boil 60ml/ 4 tbsp red or white wine in a pan until well-reduced, then stir into the finished sauce with a grating of nutmeg or black pepper.
- Add freshly chopped herbs, such as parsley, mint or dill, a few minutes before the end of the cooking time.

Making beurre manié

Literally translated as 'kneaded butter', this is a mixture of flour and butter. It can be stirred into a simmering sauce, poaching liquid or cooked dish to thicken the juices. It's an easy way to adjust a sauce or dish at the end of cooking. Any leftover beurre manié can be covered and chilled in the refrigerator for two weeks.

1 Place equal amounts of butter and flour in a bowl and knead together to make a smooth paste.

2 Drop teaspoonfuls of the beurre manié paste into the simmering sauce, whisking thoroughly to incorporate each spoonful before adding the next, until the sauce is thickened and smooth and the desired consistency is achieved.

Fixing a lumpy sauce

If a flour-thickened sauce is lumpy, don't despair – it can be corrected.

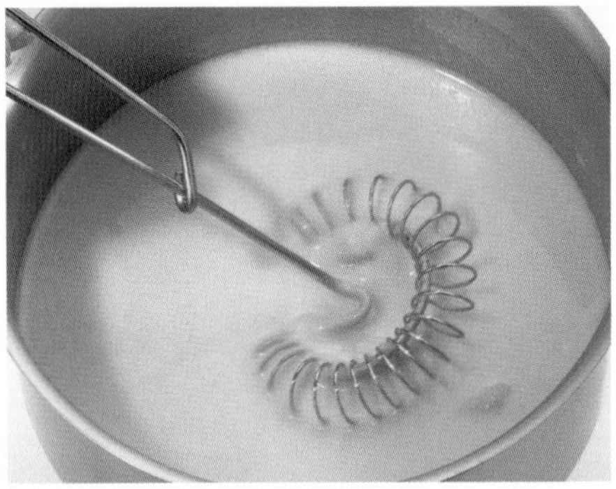

1 First, whisk the sauce hard with a light wire whisk to smooth out lumps, then reheat gently, stirring.

2 If the sauce is still not smooth, press it through a sieve (strainer) with a spoon. Reheat gently, stirring.

3 Alternatively, process the sauce in a food processor until smooth. Reheat gently, stirring.

Keeping a sauce hot

1 Pour into a heatproof bowl and place over a pan of very gently simmering water.

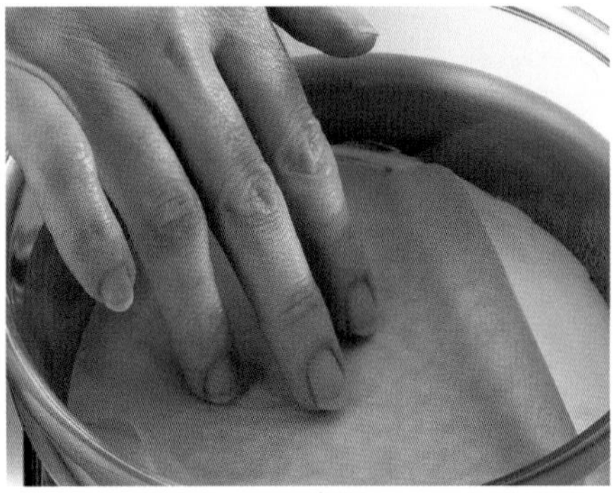

2 To avoid a skin, place lightly oiled baking parchment on the sauce.

Degreasing a sauce

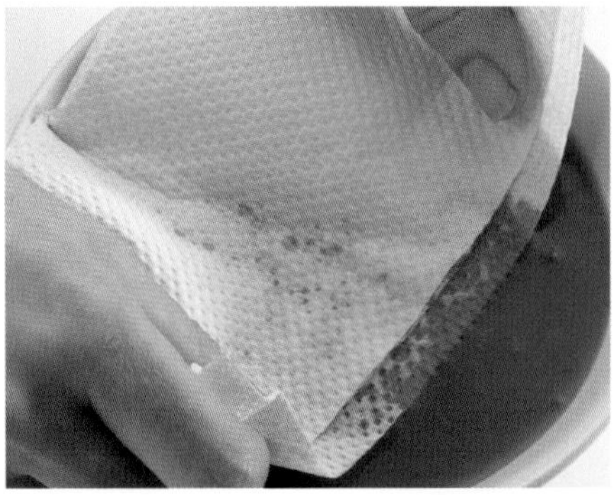

Remove any fat from a hot sauce or gravy with a spoon. Drag the flat surface of a piece of kitchen paper over the surface to absorb grease.

Making a roux-based brown sauce

The base for many sauces for meat, brown the onions and vegetables before adding flour. The fat can be butter and oil, or dripping. Butter alone is unsuitable as it burns easily at high temperatures. Use about 30ml/2 tbsp oil and 25g/1oz/$^1/_4$ cup flour to 600ml/1 pint/2$^1/_2$ cups brown stock. At the last moment, stir in 15g/$^1/_2$ oz/1 tbsp chilled butter.

1 Melt the fat and fry 1 chopped onion until soft and brown. Sprinkle on the flour and stir over low heat for 4–5 minutes, until a rich brown.

2 Take off the heat and gradually stir in the liquid, either hot or cold. Return to the heat and stir until boiling. Simmer gently, stirring, for 2 minutes, until thick and smooth. Strain the sauce to remove the onions.

Deglazing for sauce

This means adding a little liquid after roasting or pan-frying to dilute rich juices into sauce. Spoon off excess fat and scrape sediment from the pan as you stir in liquid.

1 Tilt the pan and spoon off excess fat from the surface of the juices.

2 Stir in a few tablespoons of wine, stock or cream.

3 Simmer, stirring and scraping as the sauce boils. Boil rapidly until syrupy.

Making gravy

Good gravy should be smooth and glossy, never heavy and floury. It's usually best to use the minimum of thickening, but this can be adjusted to taste. Providing the meat has been roasted to rich brown, the meat juices will have enough colour. If pale, a few drops of gravy browning can be added.

1 For thickened gravy, skim off all except about 15ml/1 tbsp fat from the juices in the roasting pan. Gradually stir in about 15ml/1 tbsp flour, scraping sediment and juices.

2 Place the pan on the heat and stir until bubbling. Cook, stirring constantly, for 1–2 minutes until browned and the flour is cooked.

3 Gradually stir in the liquid, until the gravy is the desired thickness. Simmer for 2–3 minutes, stirring, and season.

Deglazed Sauces for Meat and Game

Brandy and Peppercorn: deglaze the pan with brandy or sherry, stir in cream and coarsely ground black pepper. Serve with steaks.
Red Wine and Cranberry: deglaze the pan with red wine and stir in cranberry sauce or jelly; good with game or turkey.

Deglazed Sauces for Fish

Sauce Bercy: deglaze with dry white wine or vermouth, stir in a finely chopped shallot and sauté gently until the shallot is soft and coloured. Add cream, lemon juice and chopped parsley. Excellent with fried or poached fish.

Flavour in Brown Sauce

A well-flavoured brown stock, which has been reduced by between one-third to a half, is the basis of a good brown sauce but it can also be enhanced by these flavourings.

- A handful of chopped fresh basil, chives or flat leaf parsley, stirred into the sauce just before serving, will improve the flavour and look of a basic brown sauce.
- For game or poultry, stir a little curry paste, 2 crushed cloves of garlic and 1 finely chopped onion into the roux and cook for about 5 minutes before adding the stock. Stir in some chopped fresh coriander (cilantro) just before serving.
- Add coarsely grated orange rind to a basic brown sauce for duck or game.

Vegetable sauces and salsas

Many sauces use vegetables for flavour, colour and texture. There are endless opportunities for different sauces from the basic techniques. Puréed or chopped vegetables are used for cooked sauces or fresh salsas. Vegetable sauces and salsas are often the light alternatives to classic rich sauces, and they are invariably very easy and quick to make.

Basic tomato sauce

Fresh tomatoes must be ripe and plum tomatoes are best. Canned should be plain not flavoured. Peel fresh tomatoes before using and use about 500g/1 1/4lb tomatoes instead of each 400g/14oz can in these, and other, recipes. This will make about 450ml/3/4 pint/scant 2 cups.

1 clove garlic, finely chopped
1 small onion, finely chopped
1 celery stick, finely chopped
15ml/1 tbsp olive oil
15g/1/4 oz/1 tbsp butter
400g/14oz can chopped tomatoes
handful of basil leaves
salt and ground black pepper

1 Cook the onion, garlic and celery in the oil and butter.

2 Continue cooking the onion mixture over low heat, stirring occasionally, for about 15–20 minutes or until the onions soften and colour.

3 Stir in the tomatoes and bring to the boil. Reduce the heat, cover and cook gently for 10–15 minutes, stirring occasionally, until thick.

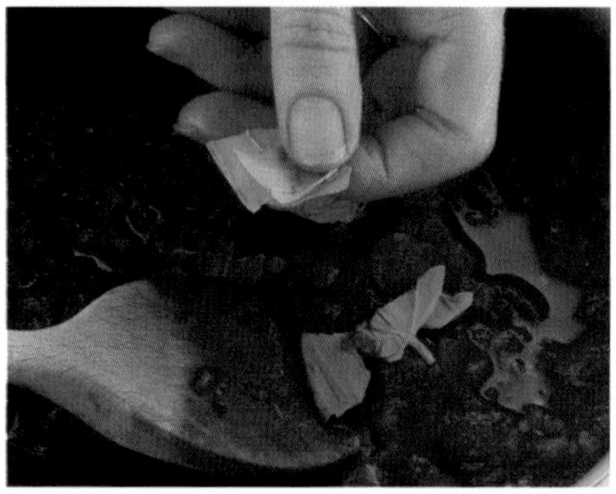

4 Tear or roughly chop the basil leaves and stir into the sauce. Adjust the seasoning with salt and pepper.

Basic soffritto

A soffritto is the base of many Mediterranean meat or tomato sauces. For basic soffritto, finely chopped onion, garlic, green (bell) pepper and celery, perhaps with carrot and pancetta, are sautéed slowly until soft and caramelized.

Quick salsa crudo

This is literally a 'raw sauce' of vegetables or fruits, and it's easy to create your own combinations of flavour. A good basic start for a salsa crudo is chillies, peppers, onions, and garlic. Serve with grilled chicken, pork, lamb or fish.

1 Peel, deseed or trim the vegetables as necessary, then use a sharp knife to cut them very finely, then dice. Try to combine texture and colour as well as flavours, and use chillies and other very spicy ingredients sparingly.

2 Put all the diced ingredients into a large glass bowl. Add 15–30ml/1–2 tbsp olive oil and a squeeze of lime or lemon juice and stir in finely chopped fresh basil, coriander (cilantro), flat leaf parsley or mint. Season to taste with salt and pepper and toss well before serving.

How to peel tomatoes

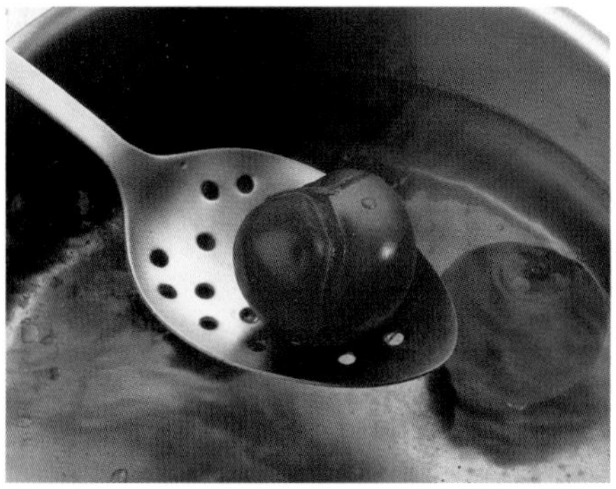

Cut crosses in the base of the tomatoes. Add to a pan of boiling water. Turn off the heat and leave for 30 seconds. Transfer to a bowl of cold water. Peel using a small knife.

Alternatively, skewer a tomato firmly on a fork or wooden skewer, and hold in a gas flame until the skin blisters and splits. When cool enough to handle, peel using a small knife.

Grilled vegetables for purées and sauces

Chargrilled vegetables are used in many sauces or salsas. Grilling on a barbecue gives full flavour, especially with peppers, aubergines (eggplants), tomatoes, garlic or onions, retaining juices while caramelizing the flesh. Alternatively roast on a baking sheet under a grill (broiler).

Roast vegetable sauce

Serve with poultry, meat or game. For a sauce with more texture, process for a shorter time. This recipe makes about 300ml/$^{1}/_{2}$ pint/1$^{1}/_{4}$ cups.

2 red or orange (bell) peppers, halved
1 small onion, halved
1 small aubergine (eggplant), halved
2 tomatoes with skins removed
2 garlic cloves, unpeeled
30–45ml/2–3 tbsp olive oil
15ml/1 tbsp lemon juice
25g/1oz/$^{1}/_{2}$ cup fresh white breadcrumbs

1 Place the vegetables and garlic cut sides down on a baking sheet. Cook under a very hot grill, or in a hot oven, until the skins are black and charred, and the flesh is tender.

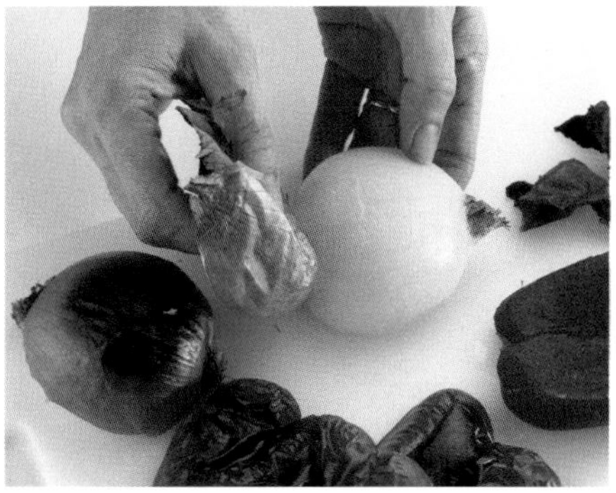

2 Remove from the heat and leave until cool enough to handle, then peel the peppers and onions.

3 Scoop out the flesh from the aubergines, and squeeze the flesh from the garlic.

4 Place all the vegetables in a blender or food processor and process to a smooth purée, adding oil and lemon juice to taste.

5 To thicken a vegetable purée, stir in a very small quantity of fresh breadcrumbs and process for a few seconds. The mixture will thicken further when left to stand.

Savoury butter sauces

The simplest sauce is melted butter flavoured with lemon juice or herbs. A more refined version uses clarified butter, which has moisture and added ingredients removed. Emulsions of butter with vinegar or other flavourings make rich beurre blanc or hollandaise sauce. Cold flavoured butters flavour and moisten hot foods, and can be shaped prettily.

Blender hollandaise

This rich butter sauce is quick and easy to make in a blender. This recipe makes 250ml/8fl oz/1 cup.

60ml/4 tbsp white wine vinegar
6 peppercorns
1 bay leaf
3 egg yolks
175g/6oz/¾ cup clarified butter
salt and ground black pepper

1 Simmer the vinegar, peppercorns and bay leaf in a small pan until reduced to about 15ml/1 tbsp. Discard the flavourings.

2 Place the egg yolks in a blender and start the motor. Add the reduced liquid through the feeder tube and blend for 10 seconds.

3 Heat the butter until hot. With the motor running, pour the butter through the feeder tube in a thin, steady stream until the sauce is thick and smooth. Season to taste with salt and pepper, and serve warm with poached fish, eggs or vegetables.

Correcting curdling

If hollandaise sauce is overheated, or if the butter is added too quickly, it may curdle. If this happens, remove it from the heat immediately, before the sauce separates.

Quickly drop an ice cube into the sauce, then beat hard until the cube melts and cools the sauce. It also helps to stand the base of the pan in a bowl of iced water while whisking in the ice cube.

Beurre blanc

This is one of the simplest sauces to make. White wine and vinegar are reduced in volume over high heat to produce an intensely flavoured sauce. Butter is whisked into the liquid to enrich and thicken it. This is a good sauce to serve with poached or grilled fish or chicken.

1 Place 45ml/3 tbsp each of white wine vinegar and dry white wine in a small pan with a finely chopped shallot. Bring to the boil and boil until reduced to about 15ml/1 tbsp.

2 Cut 225g/8oz/1 cup chilled unsalted (sweet) butter into small cubes. On low heat, gradually whisk in the butter, piece by piece, allowing each piece to melt and be absorbed before adding the next. Season the sauce to taste with salt and pepper and serve immediately.

How to clarify butter

Clarified butter is heated until the moisture evaporates and ingredients other than fat (for example, salt) separate out, leaving clear rich fat. Clarified butter, ghee in Indian cooking, keeps well and can be heated to higher temperatures than ordinary butter without burning. It can be used for sautéing, and in sauces it gives a mild flavour and a high gloss. There are two main methods of clarifying.

Heat the butter in a pan with an equal quantity of water until it melts. Remove from the heat and cool until the butter sets. Carefully lift out the fat, discarding water and solids.

Alternatively, melt the butter over low heat. Cook gently until it stops spitting and a sediment forms. Skim off scum. Strain through a sieve (strainer) lined with muslin (cheesecloth).

Making savoury butters

Flavoured butters can be shaped or piped decoratively to serve with steaks or poached or grilled fish.

To make a herb-flavoured butter, finely chop your choice of fresh herbs. Beat the butter until softened then stir in the herbs to mix evenly.

Making shaped slices

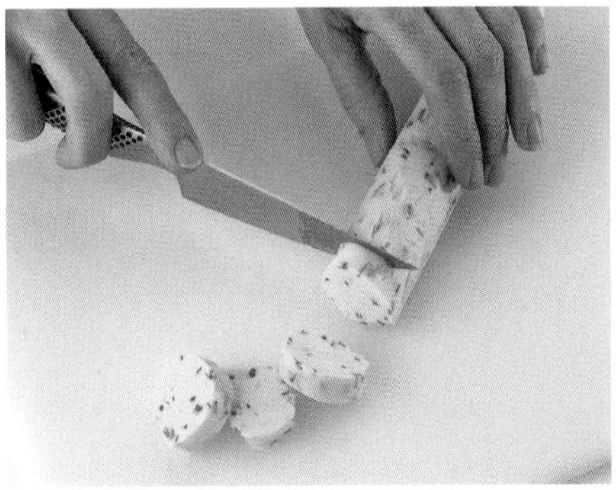

To make butter slices, chill the softened herb butter lightly. With your hands, roll the butter into a long sausage-shape and wrap in baking parchment or clear film (plastic wrap). Chill and cut off slices of the butter as required.

Piping butter

Soften the butter before filling the pipe then, using a star nozzle, squeeze on to baking parchment.

Making shaped butters

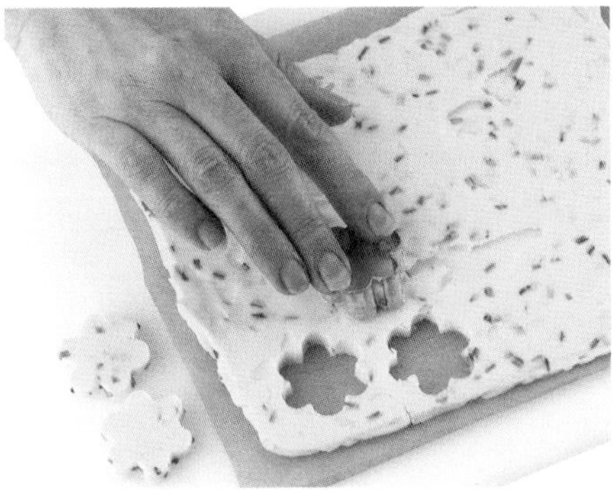

Chill lightly, then roll out the butter between sheets of baking parchment. Chill until firm, then remove the top sheet and stamp out small shapes with a cutter.

Flavourings for Savoury Butters

Flavoured butters can be rubbed or spread on meat before roasting, grilling (broiling) or barbecuing; used on foil-wrapped fish; or used for hot breads instead of garlic butter.

- Finely chopped herbs, such as chives, parsley, coriander, basil, dill, mint, thyme or rosemary. Use one herb or a combination and add as much as the butter will comfortably absorb, or to achieve the required texture and flavour.
- Finely grated lemon, lime or orange rind and juice.
- Chopped canned anchovy fillets.
- Finely chopped gherkins or capers.
- Crushed, dried chillies or finely chopped fresh chillies.
- Crushed, fresh garlic cloves, or roasted garlic purée.
- Ground coriander seeds, curry spices or paste.

Savoury egg sauces

Eggs are widely used for thickening and enriching sauces, or for making an emulsion, such as mayonnaise. Freeze any spare egg yolks for sauces: stir in a pinch of salt or sugar before freezing to prevent them from thickening.

Mayonnaise

Hand-whisked mayonnaise is smooth, glossy and perfect with delicately poached salmon or a chicken salad. The choice of oil depends on taste: extra virgin olive oil is often too strong. It's a good idea to use either light olive oil or half olive oil with half sunflower oil, or another lighter-flavoured oil. All ingredients should be at room temperature for a good sauce and to help avoid curdling. This recipe makes about 300ml/1/2 pint/1 1/4 cups.

2 egg yolks
15ml/1 tbsp lemon juice
5ml/1 tsp Dijon mustard
300ml/1/2 pint/1 1/4 cups light olive oil
salt and ground black pepper

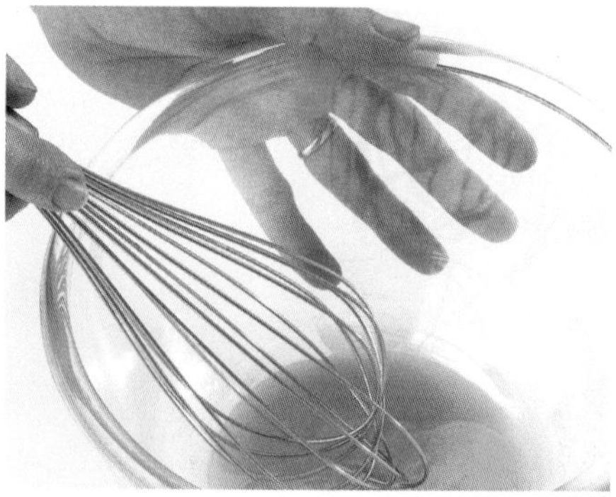

1 Place the egg yolks, lemon juice, mustard, salt and pepper in a bowl and beat the mixture until it is smooth and evenly combined.

2 Pouring with one hand and whisking with the other, add the oil very gradually, making sure that each drop is whisked in before adding more.

3 Once a thick emulsion has formed, the oil can be poured faster, in a fine, steady stream, whisking until the mixture becomes smooth and thick. Season to taste.

Blending mayonnaise

A food processor or blender will speed up the process of making mayonnaise. Use a whole egg instead of the yolks.

Process the egg and flavourings for a few seconds then slowly pour in the oil through the feeder tube in a thin, steady stream with the motor running, until the mixture forms a smooth, creamy texture.

Correcting curdling

If oil is added too quickly, the mayonnaise will separate; this can be corrected if you stop as soon as the mixture begins to separate. Break a fresh egg yolk into a clean bowl. Gradually whisk in the separated mayonnaise, a small spoonful at a time, whisking constantly until it thickens. Keep going until all the mixture is used.

Mayonnaise Variations

Spicy Mayonnaise: add 15ml/1 tbsp mustard, 7.5–15ml/1 1/2 tsp–1 tbsp Worcestershire sauce and, if you like, a dash of Tabasco sauce.
Green Mayonnaise: combine 25g/1oz each of parsley and watercress sprigs in a blender or processor. Add 3–4 chopped spring onions (scallions) and 1 garlic clove. Blend until finely chopped. Then add 120ml/4fl oz/1/2 cup mayonnaise until smooth.

Safety Note

It is recommended that pregnant women, young children, elderly people or those in ill-health should avoid eating uncooked eggs.

Sweet egg sauces

Eggs are often used to make rich and creamy sweet sauces, such as fine pouring or thick and creamy custard.

Custard sauce

Crème anglaise is traditional vanilla pouring custard sauce. It is quite different from custard made with cornflour (cornstarch) or custard powder – thinner, richer and more delicate. As well as being served as a classic sauce, either warm or cold, crème anglaise is often used as the base for creams or ice creams. It may be enriched by using cream instead of milk, or flavoured with liqueurs. This must be heated slowly and gently or it will curdle. This recipes makes about 400ml/14fl oz/1 2/3 cups.

300ml/½ pint /1¼ cups milk
1 vanilla pod (bean)
3 egg yolks
15ml/1 tbsp caster (superfine) sugar

1 Heat the milk and vanilla pod until just boiling, then remove from the heat. (To intensify the flavour split the pod lengthways.) Cover and leave to infuse (steep) for 10 minutes then strain into a clean pan.

2 Beat the eggs and sugar lightly and pour in the milk, whisking.

3 Heat gently, stirring, until the custard thickens. Remove from the heat and pour into a jug (pitcher).

Correcting curdling

At the first signs of curdling, plunge the pan base into cold water. Whisk in a teaspoonful of cornflour (cornstarch) smoothly, then reheat.

Sabayon sauce

Whisk 1 egg yolk and 15ml/1 tbsp caster (superfine) sugar per portion in a bowl over a pan of simmering water. Whisk in 30ml/2 tbsp sweet white wine, liqueur or fruit juice, for each egg yolk. Whisk until frothy and the sauce holds the trail of the whisk. Serve immediately or whisk until cool.

Baked custard

A classic partner for cooked fruit. Preheat the oven to 180°C/350°F/ Gas 4. Grease an ovenproof dish. Beat 4 large (US extra large) eggs, a few drops of vanilla extract and 15–30ml/1–2 tbsp caster (superfine) sugar. Whisk in 600ml/1 pint/ 2½ cups hot milk. Strain into the prepared dish. Place in a roasting pan. Pour in warm water to half fill the tin. Bake for 50–60 minutes.

Classic dessert sauces

As well as the popular custards and flavoured white sauces, quick and easy dessert toppings can be made almost instantly from ready-made ingredients, and these are ideal to serve over scoops of ice cream. They could also be served with pancakes.

SPEEDY SAUCES FOR TOPPING ICE CREAM

Lots of store-cupboard ingredients can be quickly transformed into irresistible sauces.

Marshmallow melt

Melt 90g/3½oz marshmallows with 30ml/2 tbsp milk or cream in a small pan. Add a little grated nutmeg.

Whisky sauce

Measure 600ml/1 pint/2½ cups milk. Mix 15ml/1 tbsp of the milk with 30ml/2 tbsp cornflour (cornstarch). Bring the remaining milk to the boil and pour a little on the cornflour mixture. Return all to the pan and heat gently, stirring, until thickened. Simmer for 2 minutes. Off the heat, stir in 30ml/2 tbsp sugar and 60–90ml/4–6 tbsp whisky.

Marmalade whisky sauce

Heat 60ml/4 tbsp marmalade with 30ml/2 tbsp whisky, until melted and bubbling. Spoon on ice cream.

Black forest sauce

Drain canned black cherries and blend a little of the syrup with a little arrowroot or cornflour (cornstarch). Add to the remaining syrup in a pan. Heat gently, stirring, until boiling and slightly thick. Add the cherries and a dash of kirsch. Use hot, warm or cool.

Chocolate-toffee sauce

Chop a caramel chocolate bar such as a Mars bar, and heat very gently in a pan, stirring until just melted. Spoon over ice cream and sprinkle with chopped nuts.

How to use Vanilla

Vanilla pods (beans) are commonly used in sweet dessert sauces, but they are occasionally used to flavour savoury cream sauces.

To get maximum flavour from the pod, use a sharp knife to slit the pod lengthways and open out. Scrape out the sticky black seeds inside and add them to the hot sauce.

To flavour sugar, bury a vanilla pod in a jar of caster (superfine) sugar. It can be used as vanilla-flavoured sugar to add to sweet sauces and desserts.

To infuse (steep) milk or cream with vanilla, heat it gently with the vanilla pod over low heat until almost boiling. Remove, cover and stand for 10 minutes. Remove the pod, rinse and dry; it may be re-used several times in this way.

QUICK SAUCES FOR CRÊPES

Rich butterscotch sauce

Melt 75g/3oz/6 tbsp butter, 175g/6oz/2/3 cups brown sugar and 30ml/2 tbsp golden (light corn) syrup in a pan over low heat. Off the heat, add 75ml/5 tbsp double (heavy) cream, stirring until smooth. If you like, add about 50g/2oz/1/2 cup chopped walnuts. Serve hot with ice cream or crêpes.

Orange sauce

Melt 25g/1oz/2 tbsp unsalted (sweet) butter in a heavy pan. Stir in 50g/2oz/1/4 cup caster (superfine) sugar and cook until golden. Stir in the juice of 2 oranges and 1/2 lemon until the caramel has dissolved.

Summer berry flambé

Melt 25g/1oz/2 tbsp butter in a frying pan. Add in 50g/2oz/1/4 cup caster (superfine) sugar and cook until golden brown. Add the juice of 2 oranges and the grated rind of 1/2 orange, and cook until syrupy. Add 350g/12oz/3 cups mixed berries and warm through. Add 45ml/3 tbsp of Grand Marnier and set alight in a safe place. When the flames have died, spoon the syrup over the crêpes.

Presentation Ideas

When you've made a delicious sauce for a special dessert, why not make more of it by using it for decoration on the plate, too? Try one of the following simple ideas to make your sauce into a talking point. Individual slices of cakes or tarts look especially good like this.

Marbling

Use this technique when you have two contrasting sauces of similar thickness, such as a fruit purée with custard or cream. Spoon alternate spoonfuls of the sauces into a bowl or on to a serving plate, then stir the two sauces lightly together, swirling to create a marbled effect.

Yin-Yang Sauces

This is ideal for two contrasting colours of purée or coulis. Spoon one sauce on each side of a serving plate and push them together gently with a spoon, swirling one around the other, to make a yin-yang shape.

Drizzling

Pour a smooth sauce or coulis into a jug (pitcher) with a fine pouring lip. Drizzle the sauce in droplets or a fine wavy line on to the plate.

Piping Outlines

Spoon a small amount of fruit coulis or chocolate sauce into a piping (pastry) bag fitted with a plain writing nozzle. Pipe the outline of a shape on to a serving plate, then spoon in sauce to fill the inside.

Feathering Hearts

Flood the plate with a smooth sauce, such as chocolate sauce. Drop in small droplets of pouring (half-and-half) cream from a teaspoon at even intervals. Draw a knife through the cream, to drag each drop into a heart.

Fruit sauces

From the simplest fresh fruit purée, to a cooked and thickened fruit sauce, there are hundreds of ways to add flavour to puddings and tarts. The addition of a little liqueur or lemon juice can bring out the fruit flavour and prevent discoloration. Some fruit sauces, notably apple and cranberry, also partner meat and poultry, and fruit salsas can cool spicy dishes.

A delicious fruit coulis will add a sophisticated splash of colour and flavour to desserts and ices. It can be made from either fresh or frozen fruit, in any season. Soft fruits and berries such as raspberries, blackcurrants or strawberries, are ideal, and tropical fruit, such as mango and kiwi, can be quickly transformed into aromatic coulis. A few drops of orange flower water or rose water add a scented flavour, but use sparely – too much will overpower delicate ingredients.

Strawberry coulis

1 Wash a punnet of strawberries. Use a sharp knife to remove any hulls from them. Place the hulled strawberries in a blender or food processor and process until smooth.

2 Press the purée through a fine sieve (strainer) to remove the pips (seeds) or any fibrous parts and create a silk-smooth coulis. Sweeten the coulis to taste with icing (confectioners') sugar, and if necessary add a squeeze of lemon or lime juice to sharpen and intensify the flavour.

For cooked peeled fruit, such as boiled blackberries, mash the fruit with a potato masher for a coarser purée.

Peach sauce

Purée a 400g/14oz can of peaches in light syrup, together with their juice and 1.5ml/$^{1}/_{4}$ tsp of almond extract in a blender or food processor. Transfer the purée to a jug (pitcher) and chill in the refrigerator before serving with sponge puddings, tarts, ice creams or mousses. This can be made with other canned fruit.

Passion fruit coulis

This coulis is superb with skewered fruit. For example, cut 3 ripe papayas in half and scoop out the seeds. Peel them and cut the flesh into chunks. Thread the chunks on to bamboo skewers.

1 Halve eight passion fruit and scoop out the flesh. Purée in a blender for a few seconds.

2 Press the pulp through a sieve and discard the seeds. Add 30ml/2 tbsp of lime juice, 30ml/2 tbsp of icing (confectioners') sugar and 30ml/2 tbsp of white rum. Stir well until the sugar has dissolved.

3 Spoon some of the coulis on plates. Place the fruit skewers on top. Drizzle the remaining coulis over the skewers and garnish with a little toasted coconut, if you like.

Chocolate sauces

Enduringly popular, chocolate sauces range from simple custards to richly indulgent versions combined with liqueur or cream. They can be served with ice cream and other frozen desserts, but are also delicious with a wide range of puddings. Liqueurs can be chosen to echo the flavour of the dessert, and coffee, brandy and cinnamon all go well with chocolate.

The best method of melting chocolate is in a double boiler or in a bowl over a pan of hot water. Never allow water or steam to come into contact with the chocolate as this may cause it to stiffen. Overheating will also spoil the flavour and texture. Plain (semisweet) chocolate should not be heated above 49°C/120°F, and milk or white chocolate not above 43°C/110°F.

For sauce recipes where the chocolate is melted with a quantity of other liquid such as milk or cream, the chocolate may be melted with the liquid in a pan over direct heat, providing there is plenty of liquid. Heat gently, stirring until melted.

Cocoa Solids

The more cocoa solids chocolate contains, the more chocolatey the flavour will be. Plain chocolate may have between 30–70 per cent of cocoa solids. Plain dark (bittersweet) chocolate has around 75 per cent, so if you're aiming at a really rich, dark sauce, this is the best choice. Milk chocolate has 20 per cent cocoa solids. White chocolate contains no cocoa solids, so strictly speaking it is not a chocolate at all, but gets its flavour from cocoa butter.

Creamy chocolate sauce

Place 120ml/4fl oz/½ cup double (heavy) cream in a pan and add 130g/4½oz chocolate in pieces.

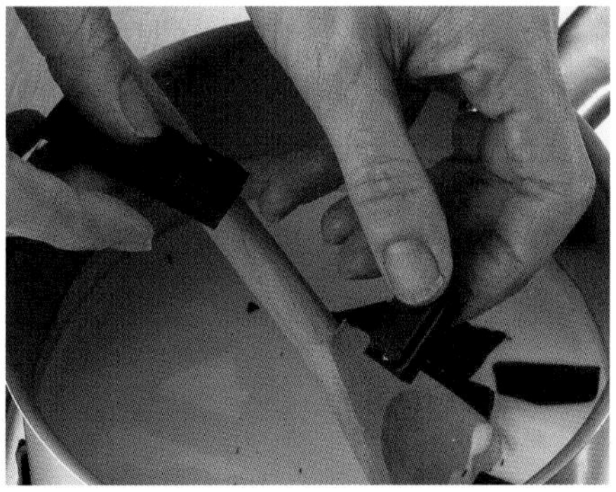

Stir the mixture over low heat until the chocolate pieces melt. Serve warm or cold.

BELOW: *from top: white chocolate, dark chocolate, and milk chocolate*

Chocolate custard sauce

1 Melt 90g/3½oz plain or dark (bittersweet) chocolate in a bowl over a pan of hot water.

2 Heat 200ml/7fl oz/scant 1 cup crème anglaise until hot but not boiling and stir in the melted chocolate until evenly mixed. Serve hot or cold.

Chocolate brandy sauce

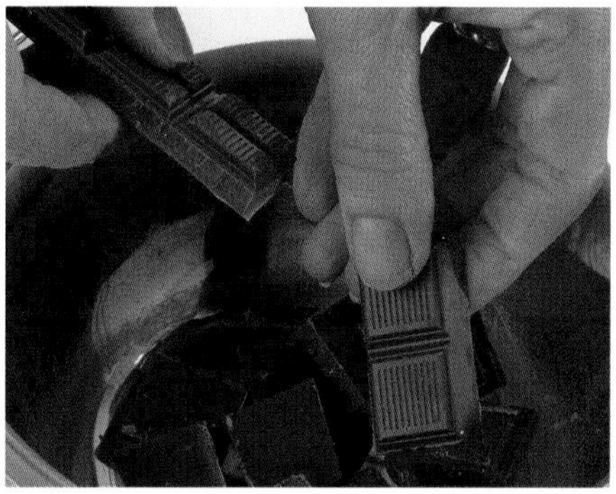

1 Break 115g/4oz plain or dark chocolate into a bowl. Place over a pan of hot water to heat gently until melted.

2 Remove the melted chocolate from the heat and add 30ml/2 tbsp brandy and 30ml/2 tbsp melted butter, then stir until smooth. Serve immediately while hot.

Marinades and dressings

Marinades can be savoury or sweet, spicy, fruity or fragrant, to flavour or enhance all kinds of foods. They're also useful for tenderizing; moistening during cooking; and as the basis of a sauce to serve with the finished dish.

Oil-based marinades

Choose an oil-based marinade for low-fat foods, such as lean meat, poultry or white fish, which may dry out during cooking. Oil-based marinades are especially useful for grilling (broiling) and barbecuing, and at their simplest consist of oil with crushed garlic and chopped herbs. Add crushed chillies for a hot and spicy marinade. Do not salt marinades as this draws the juices out of food.

1 Place the marinade ingredients in a measuring jug (pitcher) and beat well with a fork to mix thoroughly. Arrange the food in a single layer in a dish and pour the marinade over.

2 Turn the food to coat evenly in the marinade. Cover and leave in the refrigerator to marinate from at least 30 minutes to several hours.

3 When ready to cook, remove the food from the marinade. Pour into a pan and simmer for several minutes until thoroughly heated, then serve spooned over the cooked food.

Wine- or vinegar-based marinades

These mixtures are best with rich foods such as game or oily fish, to add flavour, and to contrast and balance richness. Use herb-flavoured vinegars for oily fish and add chopped fresh herbs, such as tarragon, parsley and thyme for flavour.

The acid in the wine or vinegar starts the tenderizing process well before cooking. For game, which can have a tendency to be tough, leave in the marinade overnight. Add lemon juice, garlic, black pepper and herbs, and even sherry, cider or orange juice according to your preference.

Yogurt is a good marinade and can be flavoured with crushed garlic, lemon juice, and handfuls of chopped mint, thyme or rosemary for lamb or pork. For fish, use a marinade based on lemon juice with a little oil and lots of black pepper.

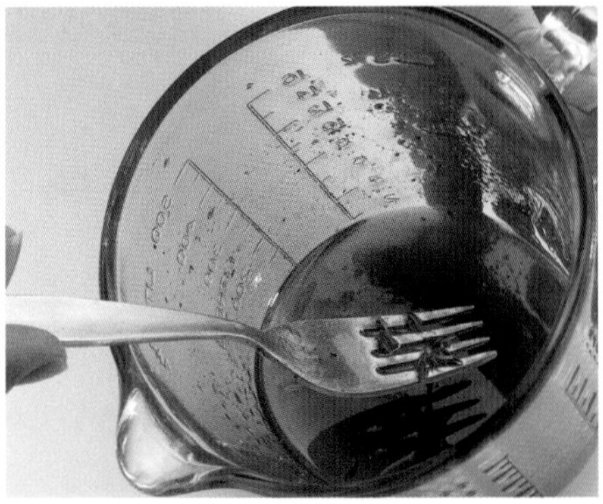

1 Measure the ingredients into a jug and beat with a fork.

2 Arrange the food in a dish in a single layer and spoon over the marinade evenly. Cover and chill for between 30 minutes and several hours, depending on the recipe.

3 Drain the food of excess marinade before cooking. If the food is to be griddled or grilled (broiled), brush with the marinade during cooking for flavour and to keep it moist.

Vinaigrette dressings

Many classic dressings, such as vinaigrette or French dressing, are based on an oil and acid mixture. The basic proportions are 3 parts oil to 1 part acid beaten together to form an emulsion. This can be done by whisking with a fork in a jug (pitcher), or the ingredients can be placed in a screw-topped jar and shaken well.

A strongly flavoured extra virgin olive oil adds personality to a simple green leaf or potato salad, but can overpower more delicate ingredients. Pure olive oil or sunflower oil adds a lighter flavour. Nut oils, such as walnut or hazelnut, are more expensive, but can add a distinctive and unusual flavour to a salad when used in small quantities.

The acid in a dressing may be vinegar or lemon juice, and this can define the flavour of the finished salad. Choose from wine, sherry or cider vinegars, herb, chilli or fruit vinegars, to balance or contrast with the salad ingredients and the type of oil. Matured vinegars such as balsamic can be strong in flavour. Balsamic has a strong flavour, because of its ageing in wooden barrels and so the basic proportions of 3 parts oil to 1 of vinegar should be amended to 5 parts oil and 2 of balsamic vinegar.

Lemon juice adds a lively tang. Other fruit juices, such as orange or apple juice can be used for a sweeter, less acid flavour.

BELOW: *Red and white vinegars*

Classic vinaigrette

To ensure the ingredients blend in a smooth emulsion, they should all be at room temperature. This recipe serves four.

30ml/2 tbsp vinegar
10ml/2 tsp Dijon mustard
1.5ml/¼ tsp caster (superfine) sugar (optional)
90ml/6 tbsp oil
salt and ground black pepper

Put the vinegar in a bowl with the Dijon mustard, salt and ground black pepper. Add the caster (superfine) sugar if you like. Use a whisk and combine well. Then slowly drizzle in 90ml/6 tbsp oil, whisking constantly until the vinaigrette is smooth and well blended. Check the seasoning and adjust if necessary.

Creamy orange dressing

This is sufficiently versatile to go with a mixed salad with orange segments and tomatoes; grilled chicken; smoked duck breasts; or chicken kebabs with rice salad. This recipe serves four.

45ml/3 tbsp half-fat crème fraîche
15ml/1 tbsp white wine vinegar
finely grated rind and juice of 1 small orange
salt and ground black pepper

Measure the crème fraîche and wine vinegar into a screw-topped jar with the orange rind and juice. Shake well until evenly combined, then adjust the seasoning to taste with salt and pepper as desired.

Variations

- Use red or white wine vinegar, or use a herb-flavoured vinegar.
- Replace 15ml/1 tbsp of the vinegar with wine.
- Use olive oil, or a mixture of vegetable and olive oils.
- Add 15–30ml/1–2 tbsp chopped herbs (parsley, basil, chives, thyme, etc) to the vinaigrette.
- Use 120ml/4fl oz olive oil and 30ml/2 tbsp walnut or hazelnut oil.

Index